WHEN ONLY THE LOVE REMAINS

Inscription

for

_____

Recipient's Name

In Loving
Remembrance of

_____

Animal Friend's Name

from

_____

Your Name

Her days are like the grass;
She flowers, like the flowers of the field;
The wind blows, and she is gone,
And her place never sees her again.

Adapted from The Book of Psalms 103,
A Psalm of David verses 15–16

A Note to My Sweet Friend

_____

_____

_____

_____

_____

_____

WHEN ONLY THE LOVE REMAINS

THE PAIN OF PET LOSS

EMILY MARGARET STUPARYK

Canadian Cataloguing in Publication Data

Stuparyk, Emily Margaret, 1953-
    When only the love remains : the pain of pet loss

Poems.
ISBN 0-9684542-0-8
    1. Pets--Death--Poetry. 2. Bereavement--Poetry.
    I. Title

PS8587.T853W44 1998   C811'.54   C98-901308-1
PR9199.3.S844W44 1998

Book design: Bruce Reimer Design

Printed and bound in Canada by
Friesens Corporation, 1999.
99 00 01 02 03 5 4 3 2 1

Dedicated to Poochie,
a precious, small, brown bunny,
who was my best friend ever.
June 10, 1992–September 16, 1997

and to all animals, loved and unloved.

Table of Contents

Foreword

Milka's beautiful collection of poems not only allows us to understand and feel her pain and sadness, but describes the ultimate bond between a human and an animal.

They say that nothing is worse than the death of a child, and our companion animals are very much like children. They depend on us for food, shelter, warmth, and love. They give us themselves in return. To care for and live with an animal, so intimately, strengthens the bond to the point where we do anthropomorphize. Who is to say what animals feel or think? I would say, more likely, the soul who has experienced and formed the relationship, not the scientific researcher.

The death of an animal does not sever the bond, as Milka's poems say so beautifully, but only changes it, in a way that further personal experiences will not be possible. The memories and feelings will remain forever.

—Dr. Catharine M. Moir, B.Sc., D.V.M.

Introduction

The poems in this book trace my journey through the first year of grief, following the death of my precious pet rabbit, Poochie. This book is about the love for an animal and the pain of losing her. It is my final farewell to her.

Many people think of rabbits as cute little animals that sit in cages and wiggle their noses. Poochie was never caged in her short life; she had full run of most of the apartment that my husband and I inhabit. Also, due to all of the attention that she constantly received, she became the most loving and affectionate animal that I have ever known in my life. I know that I became a better person for having known her and I had never experienced such a close relationship with an animal before this one.

She talked to me daily through her incredible body language, and of course, there was never a question of who was the boss. She was, of course! My husband Jim and I had many wonderful terms of endearment for her, one of which was "granny" because she always got her way, and another, "the Queen of England" because of her poise and regal manner.

There is a reason that we called her "Poochie". On her first day with us, I fed her a treat of bran cereal; she gobbled it up, proceeded to sit up on her tiny haunches and beg for more. Just like a puppy! Thus, the name "Poochie" was born, along with the start of many cherished moments and adventures.

Poochie was my very beautiful castor-coloured Mini Rex rabbit. She had a gorgeous, creamy white tummy, black gloves on her front paws, a creamy-coloured line around each brown eye and under her jaw, and the most amazing dark brown dewlap (a fold of loose skin hanging from her throat). My husband and I bought her from the Meadowood Petland in St. Vital, Winnipeg, when she was just eight weeks old; I could hold her in my cupped hands. We had just lost our precious Thumper, an eleven-and-a-half-year-old Dutchbelt bunny, from cardiomyopathy and old age.

I will never forget Dawn, the lovely, kind lady that sold Poochie to us. She had a rabbit friend as well. Dawn understood our pain of losing Thumper and our excitement in getting a new member of our family.

The bond that I shared with Poochie was one that only the heart comprehends. She was a sweet, gentle, and loving animal. We were the best of friends, soul mates; we ate, played, and slept together. Losing her created a huge void for me that no one can ever replace. Poochie taught me the greatest lesson in her short life—love to your fullest capacity each and every day.

The grief from the loss of a beloved animal is not one easily discussed in our society. This stigma that our society has, of not accepting this grief, causes many people to suppress their feelings, hindering the so-needed healing from taking place. One must go through the grieving process in order "to go on with" one's life—such a difficult thing! We grieve because we love them, miss them, want them back, hold them in the highest esteem, and will never forget them. Many people are very embarrassed by their intense feelings of grief over "just an animal", and they or others trivialize the death. This prevents them from accepting their painful feelings as normal ones and from releasing them in healthy ways.

In her book, *How To Go On Living When Someone You Love Dies*, Therese A. Rando states that "in many cases, the loss of a pet is as profound and far-reaching as the loss of a human family member. The human-animal bond can be as intense and meaningful as any human-human bond, and it must be accorded the same respect, both in life and in death."

Sorrow is the cost for having loved so deeply. I realized that losing my special friend was even more devastating than losing a family member. I never felt embarrassed by my feelings over Poochie's death—after all, they were very normal to someone who had just lost their dearest friend. You must remember that the bond is very different with an animal, and can't be put into words.

Many people resent ascribing human qualities and feelings to pets, known as anthropomorphism. I believe that animals have the same feelings as humans and they show us this every single day of their precious lives. Although my poems express much of the pain and sorrow that I experienced after her loss, they also tell the story of her life and our love for each other.

She was not just a rabbit; she was my very special "Poochie". Almost everyone has had a "Poochie" in their lives. She symbolizes the love that many cannot admit and the love that everyone should experience just once in a lifetime. This is a celebration of her glorious life and the important role that animals play in our lives. She taught me more about love and life than most people. They heal our moods when we are sad, help the lives of countless handicapped people, and teach us to love unconditionally.

My reasons for writing this book are many. Firstly, I needed to deal with my own intense grief after the sudden death of Poochie. She was like a child to me; the dearest thing to me in my life. The day after her death, I began writing about every detail of the days before, on, and after her death, over and over again. My deep feelings of shock, pain, denial, sorrow, heartbreak, loneliness, emptiness, anger, guilt, and some acceptance came out in all of these poems. My writing has helped me to remove these painful feelings and to resolve much turmoil and confusion associated with her death. I did discover, though months later, that many of my confused feelings came from the fact that one is often very disoriented and in a daze following the death of a loved one.

I was eventually able to come to terms with her death after many months of saying, "I can't believe that Poochie is dead!" Over a year after her death, I still carry some pain, although it is manageable and has diminished over time. The missing is still, at times, overwhelming, but I don't believe that one ever "completely" gets over the death of any living being, human or animal, that was loved so intensely. You learn to live with the pain.

Writing was definitely not the only way that I dealt with my pain. I cried constantly and appreciated the fact that I could cry. There is at least a teardrop for every word that I wrote. Crying releases many of the toxins produced by the body during periods of stress and is, therefore, a very healthy way to release pain. No, crying wasn't going to bring my Poochie back, but that's why I cried, because she wasn't coming back, not ever! One of the hardest things to deal with was the painful reality that I would never see her again; the permanence of this separation.

Secondly, I felt that these poems would be a fitting testimonial to my little animal friend who gave such meaning to my life. I really didn't know just how I was going to live without her; but I have, one moment at a time and one day at a time. This book is my greatest tribute to her, next to loving and cherishing her each day of her life.

Thirdly, it is my wish that these writings will give you the permission that you so desperately require to grieve for your dear pet. Perhaps they can help you to know that you are not alone in your sorrow. Sometimes, you need to immerse yourself in a sad movie, song, or book, realizing that there is no quick escape from your feelings. People need to know that just because I am bursting with happiness, doesn't mean I'm finished grieving. Also, just because I still cry, doesn't mean I'm having a breakdown.

After watching a story on television about the incredible bond that existed between a young woman with cerebral palsy and her loyal dog, I was brought to tears. A beautiful jet black Labrador jumped on the wall, turned the light switch off at bedtime, and dove into bed with his joyous owner. I recalled my life with Poochie and realized that this lady, one day, would know exactly how I feel.

May you work through your own pain and sadness as you read my poems. May you find some comfort and peace during your most sorrowful moments and perhaps, be inspired to write some special words about your own experiences with pet loss.

It is my hope that this book can help those who walk in a similar journey to mine. I know and understand the pain of pet loss and have attained some peace with the sorrow, enough to put it into words. I've found Poochie again, through my writing. Finally, real healing, I think, comes from the passing on of one's love for the departed to others who come after.

Acknowledgements

To James, my dear, loving husband, who always believed in me and in my writing; he gave me the final push that I needed to do this book and did all of the very important background work for me to bring my project to completion.

To Dr. Neil Charnock and Dr. Catharine Moir, who were Poochie's doctors all of her life. Without their expertise, support, and love, she would have never lived as long as she did.

To Donna Donald, my friend at work, who supported me from the first day that I told her about my plans. She was always ready to help, offer suggestions, and speak to others on my behalf. Thanks, Donna, for cheering me on and for sharing my enthusiasm.

To Cathy Engstrom, my close friend, who listened to my pain following Poochie's death.

To my friend, Elizabeth LaBelle, who understood my grief.

To my book designer, Bruce Reimer, whose commitment and expertise gave my "labour of love" a life of its own, and to his darling cat, Buckminster, who completely enchanted me on every visit!

And last, but certainly not least, to my precious animal friends, Bidsey and Bumper, two loving rabbits who know the true meaning of unconditional love and whose joyful escapades gave me hope when I could see none.

Books that helped me to deal with my loss:

Chernak McElroy, Susan. *Animals as Teachers and Healers: True Stories and Reflections.* New York: Random House, 1996, 1997.

Dean, Amy E. *Facing Life's Challenges; Daily Meditations for Overcoming Depression, Grief, and "The Blues".* Carson, California: Hay House, Inc., 1995.

Dickinson, Emily. *Poems,* ed. Brenda Hillman. Boston: Shambhala Publications, Inc., 1995.

Grollman, Earl A. *Living When a Loved One Has Died.* Boston: Beacon Press Books, 1977.

Kowalski, Gary. *Goodbye, Friend: Healing Wisdom for Anyone Who Has Ever Lost a Pet.* Walpole, New Hampshire: Stillpoint Publishing, 1997.

Kübler-Ross, Elisabeth. *The Wheel Of Life: A Memoir of Living and Dying.* New York: Scribner, 1997.

Montgomery, Herb, and Montgomery, Mary. *A Final Act Of Caring: Ending the Life of an Animal Friend.* Minneapolis, Minnesota: Montgomery Press, 1993.

Montgomery, Herb, and Montgomery, Mary. *Good-bye My Friend: Grieving the Loss of a Pet.* Minneapolis, Minnesota: Montgomery Press, 1991.

Nieburg, Herbert A., and Fischer, Arlene. *Pet Loss: A Thoughtful Guide for Adults and Children.* New York: Harper & Row, Publishers, 1982.

O'Connor, Joey, and Revell, Fleming H. *Heaven's Not a Crying Place: Teaching Your Child about Funerals, Death, and the Life Beyond.* Grand Rapids, Michigan: Baker Book House Company, 1997.

Rando, Therese A. *How To Go On Living When Someone You Love Dies.* Lexington, Massachusetts: Lexington Books, 1988.

Schoen, Allen M., and Proctor, Pam. *Love, Miracles and Animal Healing: A Heartwarming Look at the Spiritual Bond between Animals and Humans.* New York: Simon & Schuster, 1995.

Scot Kosins, Martin. *Maya's First Rose: Diary of a Very Special Love.* New York: Villard House, 1992.

Sife, Wallace. *The Loss of A Pet.* New York:
Howell Book House, 1993.

Staudacher, Carol. *A Time to Grieve:
Meditations for Healing after the Death of
a Loved One.* New York: Harper Collins
Publishers, 1994.

Squellati Florence, Susan. *When You Lose
Someone You Love.* Norwalk, Connecti-
cut: C. R. Gibson Company, 1997

Whitmore Hickman, Martha. *Healing After
Loss: Daily Meditations for Working
Through Grief.* New York: Avon Books,
1994.

Organizations that helped me with my loss:

Footprints On Our Hearts, Pet Loss
Support Group, Box 335, #440, 10816
Macleod Trail, S., Calgary, Alberta
T2J 5N8 Tel. (403)246-0091

The Winnipeg Humane Society For The
Prevention Of Cruelty To Animals,
Pet Loss Support Group, 5 Kent Street,
Winnipeg, Manitoba R2L 1X3
Tel. (204)989-3815

Rainbow Bridge

*Just this side of heaven is a place called
Rainbow Bridge. When an animal dies that
has been especially close to someone here,
that pet goes to Rainbow Bridge.*

*There are meadows and hills for all of
our special friends so they can run and play
together. There is plenty of food, water and
sunshine, and our friends are warm and
comfortable.*

*All the animals who had been ill and old
are restored to health and vigour; those who
were hurt or maimed are made whole and
strong again, just as we remember them in
our dreams of days and times gone by.*

*The animals are happy and content,
except for one small thing: they miss someone
very special to them, who had to be left
behind. They run and play together, but the
day comes when one suddenly stops and
looks into the distance. His bright eyes are
intent; his eager body quivers. Suddenly he
begins to run from the group, flying over the
green grass, his legs carrying him faster and
faster.*

*You have been spotted, and when you
and your special friend finally meet, you*

cling together in joyous reunion, never to be parted again. The happy kisses rain upon your face; your hands again caress the beloved head, and you look once more into the trusting eyes of your pet, so long gone from your life but never absent from your heart.

Then you cross Rainbow Bridge together...

—Anonymous

But in one respect at least I can say with a clear conscience that I have not deceived my readers— in my love for animals. I have loved them and suffered with them my whole life. I have loved them far more than I have ever loved my fellow-men. All that is best in me I have given to them, and I mean to stand by them to the last and share their fate whatever it may be. If it is true that there is to be no haven of rest for them when their sufferings here are at an end, I, for one, am not going to bargain for any haven for myself. I shall go without fear where they go, and by the side of my brothers and sisters from forests and fields, from skies and seas, lie down to merciful extinction in their mysterious under-world, safe from any further torments inflicted by God or man, safe from any haunting dream of eternity.

—Axel Munthe
    from *The Story of San Michele*

WHEN ONLY THE LOVE REMAINS

Poochie's In Heaven

You were a bright light for me,
My shining star;
Now, the light has gone out.
How will I go on!

I loved you in life and
I love you in death;
Such sadness has swept me
Away like a tidal wave;
Carried me to another place,
And now, someone else remains to grieve,
Because my pain is indescribable.

You were my strength,
My brave little soldier;
And now, the strength has gone from me too,
I miss you, so desperately.

You were everything to me,
You gave me so much joy;
And now, the angels are the lucky ones,
As they watch you romp on heaven's greens.

But I too, was lucky once,
She loved me with all her heart;
We bonded in life, and now in death,
I'll carry her wherever I go.

1

That Night

Her body slumped against her bowl,
    My eyes refused to see,
Her time was drawing to a close,
    Only God could set her free.

An agony gnawed inside her form,
    Its silence attempted to scream,
The struggle finally peaked in me,
    This fatality seemed a dream.

How many times does death knock, knock—
    An execution on the bell;
Her head was bobbing up and down—
    Cast those mean buzzards to hell.

A siren seemed to go off, then
    I pulled her close to me,
"I love you, sweet one, please don't leave!"
    Decisions subconsciously.

She'd felt that knife too many times,
    A familiar halothane;
Huge explosions in my head,
    Please terminate her pain!

Doom wrapped his blanket around me,
Still paralyzed in my space;
I stared his grimness in the face,
She'd courageously finished her race.

A final stumble, her piercing cry, then
Her toes curled awkwardly,
Her tiny head dropped on the rug,
Angels lifted her onto God's knee.

I longed to go there with her,
Overwhelming devastation;
Seasons would change before realization,
A long way from final damnation.

All Of A Sudden

All of a sudden our furry friend
Rolled over and put her head to the side;
    Cried, and died.
I'll never forget her poignant death gasp,
    When our Pooch called out,
"Goodbye, Mom, Dad!"
    Now, in that room,
    The three of us became two;
    "Sad" doesn't begin to describe our pain!
"She's all right!" I ignorantly said to my wife;
    "She'll be fine,
    It's the anaesthetic wearing off."
    Right,
    Wrong,
    All your parts are still perfect,
You still could have many more years with us;
Her head tilted to the side.
    Your heart stopped!
    Goodbye, sweet rabbit!
I gently cradled her delicate head while the
    Life sparks left her,
And felt her limp body start to grow cooler.
    I'll never forget that night,
    10:15 p.m. spoke the clock,
Or the gentle life that I and Milka will so
    dearly miss!

Goodbye, my sweet friend!
Goodbye, sweet friend!
Until our paths may once again cross.
We tried our best to help you get better, but
    It wasn't in the cards;
Set a table for us in your animal heaven,
    I'd sure like to see your
    Beautiful, black dinner gloves, once more!

Love, Dad

*(This poem was written by my dear
husband, James, my rock during this trying
time, who misses the beautiful relationship
Poochie and I shared.)*

I'll Never Again Know Her

No more rides on my shoulders,
No more cradling you in my arms,
No more stroking your beautiful body,
No more keeping me company,
No more rolling on your side in delight,
No more watching television with me,
No more Minneapolis trips,
No more playing in the cabin at
    Sioux Narrows,
No more stealing my chocolate bark,
Jujubes, or licorice,
No more snatching my banana,
No more buying your favourite red peppers,
No more squeezing fresh pineapple juice,
    No more butting my hand to pet you or
    Cover the top of your head;
    No more banging on the doormat
        at 3:30 a.m.
    No more kisses in the middle of the night,
    No more sleeping on my chest,
    No more scratching on the balcony door,
    No more dancing around your food bowl,
    No more exercising on my gym mat,
    Only extreme loneliness without you!
    No more suffering for my sweet bunny!

No more discomfort!
No more teeth operations!
No more anaesthesia!
No more Poochie!
She has gone to another place
Where grasses are greener,
Where she can hop with spring in her body,
And eat all of her food without pain,
And feel no more suffering,
And remember that I loved her!
I've given her back to you, God!
Please look after her for me,
Love her as we did in life.

The Run

I walk along the sandy beach,
    In search for peace and calm;
Alas, it's not within my reach,
    I'll coat my wound with balm.

The water tries to talk to me,
    There's comfort in its breath;
Can't you see me, can't you read me,
    It's not her time for death.

The sun has peaked, he's got a smile,
    You're strong, why can't you see?
Don't run too fast, that wretched mile,
    This path will make you free.

The wind is calling, her voice is sure,
    She says you have to know;
She loves it here, her heart is pure,
    This knowledge makes you grow.

Now keep this all inside your mind,
    Oh water, wind, and sun;
It's always there for you to find,
    So run that race for fun!

Her Fur Against My Hand

The feel of her head as she brushes my hand,
This feeling that sends me round spinning;
Always to stroke her,
Sometimes to feed her,

Often to cuddle her,
This is pure joy!
Every moment it happens,
A real live precious creature!

A gift that God gave to me,
Always so loving,
Sometimes so curious,
Often so frisky.

Will you ever know, sweet rabbit,
Just how much you are loved;
Sometimes, it's just one look,
Or a gesture, or a movement of her head.

She knows!

A Rabbit, A Fox, And Two Deer

A rabbit, a fox, and two deer,
  Some days are mottled with fear;
There's no time for whimpers or tears,
  To survive they must listen and hear.
There's so much courage inside,
  Still need a burrow to hide.

I had to kneel right down,
  To see her magnificent brown;
Her eyes were sparkling crowns,
  My smile turned into a frown,
As bunny jumped quickly around,
  Scampered away with hardly a sound.

And luck didn't come with the fox,
  A bushy white tail brushed the rocks;
I didn't even spot his head,
  All that gorgeous fur was red;
Love to see you soon next time,
  You know the pleasure would all be mine.

They stood in the bush as we drove
    to the lake,
  I called out, "two deer!"—there was
      no mistake,
Their colour ecru, their white was like snow,

Only try to imagine their grace as they
grow;
Just a moment in time, what a feeling of bliss!
Maybe see you again, but for now, there's
a "kiss!"

Can you find me a rabbit, a fox, and two deer?

My Little Palomino

She gallops towards me with a shake of
    her ears,
My little palomino!
She lowers her head and presents herself
    to me,
O little palomino!
Always so loyal and ever forgiving,
Always so gentle and ever endearing,
My darling palomino!

She's not a small pony, no phony,
As you may have thought,
A term of endearment, you see I have sought;
For my lovely creature has ears a bit longer,
And this furry pet knows that she is
    much stronger,
Much stronger, ha, ha!
And even though bunnies are famous
    for hopping,
This precious rabbit just loves to go trotting!

The Hole In My Heart

My little bear, she died one night,
And then the storm began;
It screamed and howled and raged and ripped
A hole right through my heart.

How will I fill that hole somehow,
I watch the joy ooze out
Like crimson blood;
Despair controls my future.

To fill that hole with hope and life,
Exhaustion's my constant companion;
I need to laugh, I want to feel,
Her cross I'm blessed to carry.

My goal shall be to fill my soul,
Her love can't be extinguished;
Gave of herself so generously,
Please give some valuable time.

This hole will come to fruition, no doubt,
    Fulfillment seems unrecognizable;
    Because she is dead,
    Because she is gone,
    It is done.

Poochie's Happy

Where have you gone,
My darling Poochie bear?
Where are you now,
My precious bunny bear?

Hopping in clover meadows,
Where happiness knows no bounds;
Skipping in fragrant grasslands,
Where contentment can be found.

Cavorting with your rabbit friends,
Where energy never wanes;
Grooming and licking each other,
As loving is never feigned.

But what about me,
My darling Poochie bear?
What will I do,
My precious bunny bear?

Cry rivers of sadness,
'Til finally one day,
I'll hold you in my arms,
And forever, we will stay.

Life For Life

I ask, why did she die so soon,
She lived for five short years;
　Why did she leave abruptly, when
No reason to abort.

　She sparkled like the brightest star,
The rarest of all treasures;
　When love was bursting at the seams,
My feelings, unrestricted pleasures.

　In a cage, he sat for three long years
And quietly yearned for someone,
　To love him forever, I stroked his
　　soft head;
Her journey, quite remarkably done.

　And so one life completely over,
Another happily beginning;
　God speed, precious one,
Bumper's life bells are ringing.

Oh Pain! Give Me Peace For A Moment

Oh pain, give me peace for a moment,
You haunt and torment me daily;
Pain in my heart, in my mind and my soul,
Like a hand on a pump, it crushes me.

Oh pain, you stab me like a knife—
Is this what my life's all about?
How long can I handle this suffering?
I shut my eyes in search of peace.

Such sadness I've never known,
Such pain I've never felt;
You've made a permanent home
In my heart and in my soul.

Now strength and courage are victorious,
They've become my soldiers of war;
In order to fight this battle in time,
Requires their total devotion.

Just please go away,
Won't you just disappear,
Only then will I feel
My favourite memories of her.

Like diamonds on a crystal blue lake,
And sequins on a dreamy ball gown,
No possessions on the face of this earth
Can come close to my precious bear.

What do you do when your best friend
    is gone?
How to exist in your strange empty home?
You remember the love growing
    faithfully inside,
Do whatever you can so you won't feel alone.

One Day At A Time Is Enough

What do you know of my pain,
You, who injured your leg;
What do you know of real pain,
For you, I've only disdain.

Don't tell me of your illness,
Your leg will heal in a month.
Don't bore me with your distress,
Sleep it off, you'll recover, no duress.

I don't want to hear about your problems,
You, whose car won't start;
Enough about your troubles,
The rain will help our struggles.

I don't have to handle your pain,
You don't even know of its meaning;
The pain of losing a loved one,
Your sorrow is never done.

My pain has lasted for months,
I live, but one day at a time;
Sometimes, a moment is all I can carry,
My body has grown continuously weary.

Miracles

I think that I had always hoped
    I'd bring her back one day;
Yes from the dead, you heard me right,
    A possibility, I prayed.

To hold her body lovingly,
    So firmly against mine;
So I could love her one last moment,
    And say farewell, it's time.

So I could see her in the grass,
    Amongst the shrubs and trees;
So I could watch her race and then,
    Stretch out and feel the breeze.

I know you don't believe me now,
    Just don't interfere with my scheming;
Just one more miracle and then I promise,
    To hug her goodbye while I'm dreaming.

Raindrops Only Stir The Dust

The raindrops on my windowpane,
    In the middle of the night;
Sound like she's in the room,
    Rummaging with papers under the bed.
For one precious moment,
    I think she's come back to me,
But reality clicks in,
    And I realize my imagination has
        gone wild;
Beautiful memories of happier times,
    When her glorious life was in bloom
Like all of the trees in springtime,
    Flourishing with pretty shades of green,
Just like her existence,
    Showing different shades of life;
Happiness was always around the corner,
    With sadness waiting in the wings.
But the greatest lesson of all,
    The one I carry in my heart,
Nothing holds a candle to love—
    Celebrate your wonderful days.
But I have the best of her,
    Wrapped with the strings of my heart;
Her beautiful life surrounds every moment,
    My memories of everlasting passion.

Learning To Live A Different Life

She doesn't run out to see me,
  Like so many times before;
She doesn't race circles around me,
  After darting right through the door.

Learning to live a different life
  Without her physical breath,
But how was I to know she'd have
  Such an impact after death.

Already, a relationship's begun
  With her incredible loving soul;
How else could I continue to hold
  All the sweetness and loving, He stole.

  My dearest, darling, precious friend,
  I'll always love you,
  I'll always miss you,
  I'll always remember you,

I'll always hold you in my heart.

A Vase Of Fresh Flowers

None can dispute the beauty in
A vase of fresh flowers,
Such richness in colours and class,
Whose fragrances adorn perfumes,
Can change a mood in a flash.

There's passion in a fresh bouquet;
Just linger in and hold
The joy upon another's face,
As daisies' smiles unfold.

They've given me new meaning,
Rejoicing new lives, successes;
At times, they shout a special "hi!"
To my friend, a poignant goodbye.

Her anniversary dates will cause
A moment to reflect;
The joy she gave me
In her life,
Impossible to perfect.

Her Birthday Cake

Did you ever buy a birthday cake,
For someone who has gone
    From this life to the next, distressingly,
    Such a cruel mistake.

Well, I did that on June the tenth,
My bunny would be six;
    How could I let that day go by,
    Not telling her what she meant.

"I really wish that you were here
To keep me company;
    But thank you for the happy times,
    I promise to endear."

We didn't sing the famous song
That families do so well;
    But in my heart, I sang of all
    That hadn't gone so wrong.

The Blue Exercise Mat

A toy rabbit sleeps on the softest
    Pillow that was her place;
Each night I waited for that visit,
That was her choice and space.

Approximately four in the morning,
    A knock came at my door,
A heavenly rumbling on a mat,
Protecting feet from the floor.

I awoke and called out, "She's here!"
    A leap and a thump on the mattress,
Her head on my pillow, my hand 'neath
    her dew,
Stolen hours of wonder and bliss!

I dream of the knock
    And the thump on the rug,
As I imagine her fur,
And her head, oh so snug!

That blue mat holds memories
    As the world lays asleep;
My angel had cherished
Countless welcomes, I will keep.

No Day Is A Nice Day To Die

I couldn't stop her dying,
I didn't start her living;
I wished the love on this whole earth,
Could fill the clock with mirth.

I even asked the birds that day
To sing their sweetest tune, as
All the squirrels had sensed the doom,
Would it help to fly to the moon?

The day had all the makings of
The kind that don't see funerals;
Oh, never knowing you'd have to miss
Many thousands, full of bliss.

To stop the dying, there's no such thing,
The wheels were somehow in motion;
Before I even knew what had happened,
She had curled up in God's warm hands.

God's Robe

It felt like I'd been swallowed up
By an angry, tumultuous wave,
Of torment and sadness
And debilitating pain,
Over which I had no control.

Or was it a frightening monster,
That squeezed me, oh so tight,
That my breathing had
Momentarily stopped.

Maybe, a funnel cloud,
Full of vengeance and rage
Had crashed through my window,
Encircling me with swirling dust.

Confusion set in,
Could I be mistaken?
Another Higher Power,
And I stared up in wonder.

A wave or a monster or a funnel,
It was not.
It was something more heavenly
Than I had ever imagined.

Our Father had taken my bunny from me,
He returned so that I could feel comfort;
He gently touched my hand, and then,
Her ears popped out of His robe!

I Know She Filled A Need In Me

I know she filled a need in me,
    One lacking since my youth;
So now I have to start the search
    To fill that hole with truth.
Love brings such bursting happiness,
    Caring finds essential companions,
And closeness holds the key to
    Hours of feeling free!
I want to open up my heart
    Completely so that maybe,
I'll find what I've been searching for;
    To give my life some peace.
Bidsey elongates herself on the sofa,
    Longing for some stroking;
Bumper races with a greeting,
    When the sun peeks through the curtain.
Two gentle creatures of the universe,
    That God's hands have created;
Deserving the very best of me,
    Even as my eyes fill up.

If I Could Just Go Back In Time

If I could just go back in time,
I'd visit my rabbit's life;
I'd spend those hours and those days,
Repeating every moment.
I couldn't love her any more,
That wouldn't be my goal;
Just let me touch that face again,
To hear her happy sounds.

With leisure lay upon the grass
To softly brush our toes,
And catch the sun's most gentle rays,
Just cherish moments like those.
We'd snuggle warmly beneath the covers,
No greater joy for me!
My heart had always known for sure,
She'd felt exactly like me.

I'd pet the fur upon her head,
Three licks across my nose;
"Go to sleep my precious rabbit
And dream those bunny dreams!"
Eventually, I'd sadly know,
Our time would have to end;
And then so gently, say so long,
She'd never hear goodbye!

Pictures

Perhaps I'd just gone raving mad,
    The camera's brights had flashed;
    Her fragile body needed sleep,
So ethereal and serene.

My consciousness had left me,
    A vacant cavity;
    He'd see her smile at heaven's white gate,
Death stole that pleasure from me.

The best of me had died that day,
    Perchance to leave this place;
    She stirred the clouds above me as
I languished hypnotically.

I hugged and kissed her small, limp corpse,
    Survival a fantasy;
    I even lay beside her and
My vigil had commenced.

The road stretched out beyond us now,
    And "dust to dust" she'd be;
    I gazed into her soulful eyes,
Would crying set me free.

Pink floral urn, her ashes lay
   Inside a rabbit sack;
   Her picture's always at my side,
I feel that she's come back.

I know she is immortal now,
   If only in my head;
   A part of her will never die,
In me, she's found her bed.

Oh Summer, Who Will You Love
This Year?

Summer, take your time this year,
Rest your weary bones,
Your splendour full of excellence and promise,
Holding secrets of her past;
Your gentle winds moved through her fur,
While fragrant blossoms tantalized her smell
And grasses fed her rounded tummy,
Your golden morning blessed her with
    sunbeams,
Such creamy clouds wrapped her in shade.

Oh summer, who will you love this year?
She can never feel your breezes!
She'll never again sniff your flowers!
Your sun can't warm her gorgeous face!
Even clouds can't find a reason
To float and circle the skies.
Birds mournfully telling tales of tragedy,
Squirrels whimpering "Where's she gone?"
Bunnies thumping their hind feet,
To honour their precious "queen",
All of nature with her fervour,
Nostalgically reminiscent
Of all life ended soon.

Your everlasting love,
Sweet summer of my life,
To extinguish your flame,
Death has no dominion.
You've such love for them all,
Those poor forgotten creatures;
Give them life in the heavens,
So their spirits may soar high,
Strong and joyous up above.
Don't forget your brightest sunshine,
Refreshing breezes, all you can muster,
Offer them grasses, all your greenest,
And send my love in your fanciest package.

Broken Heart

A heart that's shattered into a million pieces,
Can it be mended like one sews
A rip in his pants or blouse?
My heart won't mend in my lifetime,
Cause my bunny's not coming
Back from the dead,
Not ever!

It's the permanence that's so painful,
All it took was one thought of her sweetness,
And my troubles seemed so distant;
All I needed was to snuggle up close,
My life was perfection in motion.
I loved waking up to her animal wonders,
Surprises and adventures seemed endless,
Bunny tangos—jumping figure eights
    at my feet,
Her little paws calling
In a language we both understood,
"Can I sleep with you?"
Sheer excitement as she landed
On my chest for her favourite banana;
Catching her butterball body roll,
My heart promising to burst,
Limitations nonexistent in her joy,

Our joy,
Two hearts melted into one soul.

I'm learning to live with my broken heart,
Twisting and turning highways,
I'm in a foreign country,
The mystery remains steadfast;
The unknown that's put my life back
    into order,
Because there was a period for many
    months or so,
When most certainly even the best days
Possessed that bad feeling,
Like something was always wrong,
My life in disarray,
A table in a restaurant that couldn't be
Levelled by any number of napkins;
That feeling has dissipated into the air
Like the angry smoke that drifts into a cloud;
I'm learning to live without her
    loving presence,
I couldn't have known that I'd survive
Without my friend.

Stages Of Grief

On the dreadful night that she died,
I conceived that I'd descended
Into a deep hollow pit
Of demons and monsters and snakes;
My body lay frozen like a corpse,
Stiffening into rigor mortis.
My suffocating brain,
As death became an obsession,
A contagious disease spreading
To everyone I loved;
Wrapping its claws around me, I ate,
Slept, read, and ran with death,
As its nails pierced my transparent skin,
Poisoning me for eternity.

My feelings sterile, I gratefully
Entered a state of denial;
Playing hide and seek under the bed,
Heaven didn't own her yet.
Momentarily, she'd come flying out
With that smug look on her face;
I'd massage her gorgeous Rex fur.

Driven by sorrow and emptiness,
I would focus on
Blaming someone, anyone for this atrocity;
Even though my love for her was abiding,
I'd repeatedly criticize
My delayed decision to go to the vet;
Her gentle doctor,
Who always held her best interests at heart,
Had he made a bad decision?
And oh, my husband,
My best friend in the world was
Too far away at a music lesson to help us.

What purpose would
This destructiveness serve?
Only hurt the people who loved her,
An exercise in futility that
Could never ever bring her back to me;
I floated into a world of escape,
A state of depression.

Like on Hallowe'en night,
I wore my happy mask
For those who couldn't empathize;
My body screamed for rest
As I forced myself to run,

Hoping to elevate those endorphins;
Like a creature come to life,
My card exploded at every counter;
Sleep became a drug I craved that
Pushed the pain momentarily away,
As my memory happily
Embraced sluggishness;
Concentration soared into oblivion,
Hope dropped at my feet
Like the newspaper thrown on my porch;
Still out of control,
Crying was pounding at my heart;

A thunderstorm waiting to explode,
A reincarnation of myself,
A metamorphosis of sorts,
As a butterfly landing on a flower;
I gracefully entered this new life,
Taking nothing for granted...
No time machines to walk into,
Her jewels decorate my heart.

Grooming In A Golden Rabbit Hole

Never viewing recovery,
Never coming out of this death,
    Never to be seen on this earth again—
    The saddest day of our lives.

This fantastic belief in heaven,
Finally reunited
    With your furry friend,
    Waiting a lifetime at heaven's gate.

Impossible to go on,
Without this knowledge in the offing;
    One day I shall see you grooming
    In a golden glowing rabbit hole.

My eyes shall not cease tearing,
I shan't believe this heavenly vision,
    Of her eyes crying softly of the love
    That's come back to her.

Learn To Live With It

After months of circular,
Triangular,
And linear analyzing,
At times, a haze comes over me,
Some kind of tranquil trance;
You finally just,
Learn to live with it.

No reasons given,
No questions answered,
No answers found,
No conclusions drawn.

Just pure virgin paper,
Staring at my face;
Eyes wide open in wonderment,
Still confused and turbulent,
And again,
You have to live with it.

A voice inside me that won't be stilled,
It begins all over again;
Sometimes, it's caught in my throat,
And then it heaves like a sick child at night,
Leaving me with a sour taste in my mouth,
A bad feeling in my life.

An unwelcoming pit screams out his invite,
Dare I enter that horror-filled place;
Unlike that dreaded day, controls
    remain intact,
I pull my feet out and stand still.

The choices come at me, kind peace
    is at hand;
My breathing, so slow, eyes close shut and
    I dream
Of my blessings, they call in their love
And extinguish the fires in my heart.

Dreams Drop Out Of Heaven

How will I know
    That I'm truly moving on;
    Will I know when the trumpet
Announces my rebirth.

How will I discover the courage
    To suppress all those fears—
    To exist the rest of my life,
To endure the pain and suffering of loss.

Since sadness still drags behind me
    Like an anchor at sea;
    It shields my being,
So completely and irrevocably,
    Like a holy mantle.

Seems soothing now, and over time,
    Indeed, an essential part of me;
    Will I ever cease to embrace
Those impassioned winds flowing
    Through the very essence of me.

Like a banshee, I scream,
    No one can ever know
    The severity of this wound;

No tourniquet could stop the flow
    As blood drains out of me.

So carry on, O mighty forces—
    Don't abandon me ever;
    Please keep me safe and warm,
And carry me through your deserts,
    Where dreams drop out of heaven,
    To give my lonely heart a rest.

Pretending In The Park

Denial did knock
At such fragile walls as mine,
Not once, but twice that year,
Incredibly kind or vicious intent,
Saving me from the ravages of that pit;
Rhythmical feet, as they ran on muddy paths,
My vision, automatically clearer,
My breathing, decidedly smoother,
That stitch in my gut,
miraculously vanished.
The sky seemed clearly blue,
A cheerful sun above,
The birds sang louder,
The world was suddenly awake,
Filling my body with sheer excitement;
Her ghost called out to me,
"I'm always here and at your side!"
Insanity was taking his turn,
"Oh, are you happy to see me?"
Don't want you to know, the reality of
my grief,
I'm really all right, sweet peace is at hand,
But who do I think I'm fooling?
"Imaginary worlds forever!"
Cause she's come back,
And maybe staying awhile,

In the form of a bumpy log,
Or reincarnated into a dark brown squirrel;
    And boy did I ever crash
When this fantasy was over,
    Who'll pick up the fragments
Of my lost and dejected self;
    Who's gonna love me
When it feels like Armageddon;
    Who's gonna hold me in his arms,
When I cry for days on end;
    My knight in shining armour
Who's never left my side;
    "Cry as long as you need to,
She'll always be your brightest star."

A Stone Unturned

Just one last scream,
One final shout.
No one hears!
Close Pandora's box,
Acceptance on a crater,
Still!

A small, brown mouse squeaks in the night,
No strength in my claims,
My competence is gold—
Then why scream at all?

No tethered strings to tie,
Panic and confusion squeezed in like
     the mouse;
In striking glory, the skies exploded,
Enveloping me.

The survivors beckon to me,
Nonexistent chains on the sea's bottom;
Faces shining from the rays,
Always close at hand,
Forever unreachable.

Peace of my heart
And in my soul,
Always command me,
Shall never abandon me.

To Reconcile Death

To reconcile death
Is utterly impossible,
   To reconcile death,
So totally necessary;
   Seems at times like
No way out,
   Feels a lot like
Complete resignation.
   This virgin experience,
A complete form of love
   Held delightful moments in my hands,
Now suffocating in the depths of sorrow.
   The book of rules is lost in time,
Death being the ultimate joker;
   A birth into nothingness,
A voyage without destination.
   He stole the very best of me,
Now a wish to enter oblivion.
   Death punched a hole
Right through my breast,
   And ripped my heart clean out;
He threw it on the floor to die,
   I screamed, "Please bring her back!"
I'm drowning in a sea of tears,
   Madly struggling to catch my breath;
A cold black hand pushes on my head,

Strength draining, I succumb.
I've hit rock bottom, I hear a thump,
    Impossible to venture further;
As my vision becomes blurred and blotchy,
    I'm sightless—
Shock, I fall still deeper.
    Grief's dynamic pattern,
Fibrillation in a cardiac arrest,
    That a drug injected into my veins,
Could stupefy the senses.
    The waves are calm now,
The boat stops rocking;
    Could a million miles of sand
Bring tranquility to this tormented body.

Grief's Absent Without Happiness

Grief's absent without happiness,
A ballerina minus pointe;
A life contained in misery,
Nothing lost, losses everything.

But he whose love is immeasurable
Becomes the immediate target;
An ecru fawn in motion,
A bow straight through the heart.

Should I stay clear and let another
Have all this ecstasy;
If I should never love again,
Life's an empty, meaningless vat.

Grief and happiness, two bonded in marriage,
Like tortured Siamese twins;
Too much in common, a scalpel's blade,
Irreparable demise.

This shroud be worn in King's cloak style,
It's worth its weight in gold;
And bear it now, for one day soon,
Metamorphosed into feather down.

Gravestones

How many gravestones must I visit,
    Before my own I see;
A sudden departure, my curiosity peaks,
    To float eternally.

A million miles to reach this zone
    Of glowing transparency,
Where heavenly bodies in elusive states
    Achieve such harmony.

Could it be lovelier than our earth,
    Where emeralds grow in seas,
Identical to a jewellery box, the birds
    Hold all the keys.

Would God be waiting there for me,
    To give the final decision;
A permanence in paradise,
    A reunion of such precision.

The question burning most in me,
    Will my best loved be present;
Devotion plus obedience, I promise forever,
    O Master, your servant, so repentant.

Confronting Death

It's over now—
Her life is done.
Dress rehearsal not,
Can never turn back.

This thing that
Snuffed her from me,
Missing another chance;
Dropped from a place
Not talked about,
An uninvited guest.

I didn't chance to see him,
Only what he did to her.
These thoughts still
Sting my eyes with pins,
Firmly holding
My breath in suspension.

"How could you do this
To her life, my life,
Our life!"
At times,
Chained to a treadmill,
Slow backwards,
Fast forwards,
Still nowhere.

"You had your say,
Oh, leave us be,"
To pick up all the pieces,
Along with the remains.

Her body's vanished,
Kind peace at hand;
Her loving spirit's lasting,
Her brilliant star
In heaven's elevation,
Illuminates my soul,

And guides me to a land,
A dwelling for
Dear ones perished;
For I just need to
Close my eyes,
To hold her ever close.

The Song Of Death

Her illness didn't stop the world,
Her death, the same response;
A daunting task, merely tedious,
To fathom this disregard.

That road into my memory, and
No brighter sun was nigh;
The perfect breeze, the flowing trees,
Sweet lilacs presented bouquets.

Exuberant songbirds pierced the heavens,
Their finest performance yet;
And all my favourite furry friends,
A blurry race in action.

My eyes were stunned, I pondered why
Their joy held such esteem;
With stone cold heart and heavy feet,
Dragged circles round the quarry.

No knowledge of my state of mind,
Well hidden with a veil
Of instant paste I'd lacquered on,
To gratify the masses.

To hide these feelings from oneself,
Exhibits extreme heresy;
The soul becomes the devil's ground
And wars begin their plight.

A heart that can't be stilled at all,
A voice that won't be silenced;
When all is done that could have been,
Just say, "It isn't so!"

Inevitably, an aging weariness,
When all abruptly ceases;
At last, an anguished voice cries out,
"I can't do this much longer!"

This song of death, it must be sung,
'Til all its breath exhausted;
And in its place, the angels sing,
Praising memories, welcoming rebirth.

Her Legacy

I've left that other life behind,
    The one with her and me;
Where never could I so imagine,
    My bear, I'd fail to see.

But try I have with all my strength,
    To carry on some way;
That knowing very well for sure,
    Find happiness one day.

My friend, she isn't very far,
    She's always at my side;
And has the best place in my heart,
    That carries a shimmering star.

I miss her friendship every day,
    I miss the times of best;
I'll look for these in other bears,
    Only then, my heart shall rest.

I'll always love my tender bear,
    Such kindness in her face;
Her love remains a constant force,
    It's priceless in this case.

I'll bear the pain as best I can,
   The months will turn to years,
As thoughts of her entire life
   Bring ending to my fears.

Perhaps one day, I'll surely feel
   Such happiness again;
But now, sit still and hold on tight,
   To blessings in my sight.

The Book

I'm contemplating
A book for you,
My precious bunny bear;
I offer you
This wondrous gift,
My greatest,
Not for sure;
You taught me about
The power of life,
Its happiness and
Its pain,
The unconditional love
You gave,
Cannot be repeated.

This important decision
To write these poems,
Has changed my life
For sure.
But you're the one
That made me see,
Live each day
To the fullest.

This journal's become
My closest friend,

So I might spill my tears.
And you,
Consistently with your love,
Gave me the final key.

I wish I didn't have to,
Need to write,
I'm driven by death
And my sorrow;
I wish these words
Need no release,
Of course,
She'd be alive.

How many of us do
Love our feelings;
I nurture them,
They're mine.
Through analyzing
All my thoughts,
I reveal my
Hidden secrets.

I'm Assaulted By The Absence
Of Her Presence

I'm assaulted by the
Absence of her presence,
An incessant longing captures me,
Like a prisoner without hope of escape;
A lifelong sentence for
The indelible crime of loving.

A fantastic chest of memories
That coat my entire being,
Two bodies in communion,
A blending of our souls;
Imbedded in my mind,
Her vigour and love of life,
At times, I've visions of her,
When life so bloomed within.

Expressive eyes, a pouty mouth,
A fluffy and pendulous dewlap,
That swayed and bounced
With every hop,
She groomed it like her baby;
Her rolls were magic to our eyes,
Exposed a creamy tummy,
That look, impossible to resist,
Her capacity to steal your senses.

From all the smallness in the world,
Her power commanded your moment,
So pure and precious, and yet so brief,
A love so foreign to asunder;
Rapidly, disease so viciously attacks
The life that gave you life,
Like poison from a venom snake,
Life oozing from the hole.

Stabs of insanity, my instant friend,
Reality thrust from immediate reach,
To preserve that life inside a box,
To administer it as a balm;
To let such madness enter me,
A thought, so utterly absurd;
Unless you saw the love that was,
So sweet shall always be.

There's silence in the dead of night,
A desperate wish for embracing
Of dreams, that transform me in time,
Two lives that burst in unison.

Her Final Dance

Want to stop thinking,
Need to stop conceiving,
Can't stop reviewing,
Events of her demise.

A wish, perhaps had not,
A chair at her finale;
Her final dance,
No curtain call,
No encore;
With knowledge instrumental,
A sleep with much resistance.

Missing severely intensified,
Domination of the hours,
Surreptitiously steal a glimpse,
Embedded to the infernal
Merry-go-round.

Not so merry, is it?
At times, defies all words;
To simplify her final breath,
A considerable misjudgement.

Ten Months

Ten months inside a milestone,
A determinable eternity,
A lifetime, maybe several,
Since death was not foremost.

Submerged in silent rivers,
A vacuum resisting description;
Pure love not overlooked,
Ageless joys dispersed beneath dirt.

An expansive love,
Rich in bosom companionship;
A bond inexplicable,
Betwixt a girl and her friend.

In popular stories
That children hold dear,
Comes one straight from heaven,
Wrapped in rainbows and
Sprinkled with stardust.

Dusty

The girl that sold us Poochie,
An intimate tale to tell;
Three years went by,
A tearful Dawn,
Not neglecting any raindrops,
God's affection never wanes.

Her pain distinct,
But clearly apparent;
This love on her sleeve,
I wept aloud.

Dusty's pure white body
With soft grey colours,
An exceptional creature,
No imagination required.

Repetition always,
Inadequacy outstanding;
Lingers a prevalent question,
Bee's honey on a bear's paw.

What if, why not,
And on it goes;
The treacherous hill climbing,
No deviation permitted.

A detour from this sorrow,
An uproar of all proportions;
The cruelest injustice,
A transgression to mankind.

When all the dead are buried,
And all the loved are gone;
No kinder known memorial,
Bestowing love during life.

Pain Is Silent

Pain is silent,
Perfectly still,
A gaping hole, wide open,
No closure, zigzag scars.

Pain finds your soul
Riding life's madness;
In an instant,
Disappearance of
Your faculties.

A howling sea storm,
Survival of the fittest;
Greedy, impatient waves
Surround your carcass;
The sea,
A vast blue mausoleum.

Trapped in a sandstorm,
Gravelly eyes,
Heavy footprints;
Blindness first,
Rapidly sinking,
So deep and never found.

Pain's only kindness,
When it leaves your
Tortured mind and spirit—
A solitary gift.

I don't know how
To heal myself,
Sweet pain, take leave so I
Can feel my dear, sad heart beat life
And gently rejoice once more.

Show understanding for my need
To chain you to the mound,
And visit you, don't visit me,
Just trust your faithful friend.

The Dream

Chasing demons daily,
An excruciating pastime,
No haven found on earth,
Escaping ghosts of past;
A witch upon her stick at night,
Beneath the silvery moon;
Obscenities screamed,
Barely deciphered,
Shivers down my spine.

A black haze ragged gown,
Fantastic pointed hat,
Competitive with that warted nose,
A snake-like finger stabs me
In the chest,
Repeatedly 'til I drop
Inside a mud-filled tunnel,
So dark, no sign of light.

Then,
Lucifer himself appears,
Red, shining, neon eyes,
I blink but once,
A sticky frog clogs my throat;
Feet nailed to the ground,
Private crucifixion—
Unspeakable tortures,
This is hell!

An illusion of peace,
Floating into subconsciousness,
Pain eludes my every nerve,
Continuous flashing lights
Like steel across my face;
I'm in and out of death,
Struggles ensue,
The ultimate decision,
Destination unknown.

Unexpectedly, a body spasm,
Twitching back and forth;
Morning sky, rising shock,
Bedroom floor around me,
Images like whirligigs,
A speeding underground,
Profusely sweating,
A rapid heartbeat,
Nightmare terminated.

Landing in bed,
A cocoon of covers,
Such happy sweat inside;
At last,
With safety net around me,
Life's ever abundant.

Different Kinds Of Grief

I held her body
One last time,
How could this come to be;
With all the love I gave in life,
To view her spirit free.

Do others have this kind of pain,
A heavy heart, forlorn;
Do others say "Just let it go,"
Their choice is not to mourn.

It's been said that one can't know,
Until their time draws near;
A shaking of the shoulders and
A filling up of tears.

I'd known of death long time ago,
A different kind of stream;
Real love was just a fantasy,
Occurring in my dreams.

A wish for love I'd never had,
A kinder, gentler world;
And happiness, a distant vision,
So constantly being hurled.

Grief for Mom still has its place,
     Although I've gained some breath;
Because there was a screaming absence,
     And not just in her death.

No such thing as pure honesty,
     My feelings had been raped,
And buried many years ago,
     In time, they'd need escape.

So sad to die without the love,
     This shouldn't be condoned;
But nothing's worse in this whole world,
     Than dying all alone.

At least I know when I am called
     To leave this blessed place;
I'll know the joy of loving some,
     And experienced the greatest race!

Why

All these months gone by,
And I still must ask why
All of the time;
Even though with more certainty,
No answers in sight,
Most of the time.

A horror incomprehensible,
Totally senseless in its nature;
Such a torment without reason,
So required to move on.

Questions continuously gnaw at me,
Like a dog to his bone;
Can't let go, so disturbing,
Ask the dog, he should know.

As though this unreachable answer
Would somehow bring her back;
To gain what from this inquisition,
But an answer to a question.

Are such queries really lacking,
The whys, why nots and hows;
Or a fiercely intense longing,
That drives you to
A world of dementia.

To have her right beside me,
Brown eyes perpetually smiling,
Soft snout persuading me
To gently run my happy hand
Through her rich dark coat.

Such A Chill In The Air

Such a chill in the air,
Strangely, not in the room;
My poor heart has gone cold,
November's frost has come soon.

A smooth frozen river,
A friendship with my skates;
Pray my heart could be melted,
Joyous water of our spring.

As dense as the smoke
Of a brush fire burning;
In hopes to get through
All this blackness and soot.

A fresh lovely garden,
I'll stroll through some day;
Is this excellence an omen,
Of a heart's arrival home.

The Past Has Come Back

Today, I'm swallowed up
By unrelenting emotions,
No comfort found in ancient devices;
Perhaps, there's no breath
As I contemplate this world.

The past has come back,
As though it's just happened;
Despondent and feeble,
Let me retire now to dream,

Of those beautiful days,
When my beatitude was new;
And no days could be counted
That would foul up a mood.

A sadness that does weave,
A wretched tapestry cross my skin,
And promises to persist,
Much longer than I can stand.

God Was There

No feelings of complacency,
When life sang loud and clear;
Incessant laughter around the bend,
As chasing, racing, cuddling and loving
Filled a pool of daily celebrations.

While safe in the recesses of my mind,
A dread that sleep would come;
When chronic illness still persisted,
Our love would guard her
Or so I thought—
The spider's web was done.

Some bluebirds sang her final song,
As portentous clouds, so black,
Hovered closer, then mushroomed over;
For when her whiskers twitched no more,
"He" had to hold me up.

Everywhere

Not anywhere,
Yet everywhere,
An empty red throne,
Curled up and sweet.

A spot by the window,
Her ghost lays quietly,
At times, moves stealthily
Through the room,
Searching for me.

I look no longer;
She's in every animal
I love,
In every animal I see,
Every animal I touch.

Living all the rest of my days,
Without her, seems forever;
Optimism lies on the wings
Of a dove,
To carry me safely home.

Madness

Madness came
Disguised as death,
Seemingly rash and sudden,
Moving with unstoppable force,
Not on this act of mine;
Slow rotation, O flowered urn,
In resurrection style.

A calamitous bolt,
A momentous mistake,
An unforgivable impropriety,
Dehydration of our rose.

Your greedy God,
What purpose in snatching
Her from our reach;
His breath on my nightmare,
Unkind and unjust.

Not rectifiable,
This rotten course of events;
The old are left to grieve,
"Only the good die young,"
Billy Joel once sang.

Praising Loves Still In Place

We all live for love,
And some love to live,
Emerald green blades of grass,
Iced with morning's sweet dew.

Richly velvet, upright bulrushes
Rhythmically dancing in the breeze,
And those sweet black-eyed susans
With their darling daisy friends,
Speaking volumes to me.

Merganser mom leads her babies,
So protectively above the deep;
And the loon, so elegant afloat,
Sings our lullabies to sleep.

When my eyes start to glisten
Mini rivers down my face;
It's the loves that I've lost,
Praising loves still in place.

Summer's Lazy Days

Summer's lazy days
Puncture me with reminders,
Of an unconditional love,
God's gentle few, my precious rose.

I seized the majesty enveloping me,
So affectionately,
Gently squeezing my sensibilities;
The black-eyed susans quietly
Whispering secrets
That only I could comprehend.

A pebbled surface beneath my feet,
Boundless baby blue wrapping
My shadows;
Ribbons of white to shield the sun,
A splendid archway of foliage.

Imprisoned with my thoughts,
A life sentence from God;
Bad things don't just happen
To other people,
In life's natural rhythm,
Nature gives
And she takes.

Barely escaping suffocation,
I fear the worst to come;
Is time the world's great healer,
Or just the saying goes.

The Hummingbird

I can't read anymore,
I can't write anymore,
My eyes are tired,
But their sting won't leave me alone;
The tears wash away the glue my
    eyelids crave.
I think I'll wait for
The little hummingbird's buzz tomorrow,
To start a new day, a different day.
I'll welcome the cool sunrise on the lake,
So rosy and fair, and full of promise.
Summer breezes play in and around me,
A happier day, I hope.
The past is still there,
Tiled with memories, sweet and sad.
A good friend of mine once said
That he'd met many dishonest people,
But never once, a dishonest animal.
They bear their burdens silently,
And silently they say goodbye,
Without ceremony;
The sparrow knows not its own beauty.
When the good Lord says:
"That's all,"
That's all.
We honour them by loving them,

By respecting their natural beauty
And their well-being;
Saying goodbye
With a teary eye,
Reflects love with those salty drops;
Can we ever leave the sad parts behind,
Alas, a rock to forever roll, I think.
Indeed, today will ride on its shoulders,
And tomorrow, the beginning of eternity.
It is put to rest a day at a time,
As it tallies yet another day.
Just one more line to finish,
And let it be a joyous scribble.
My pen won't move,
It must, meddlesome quill;
"I must go now," it writes,
"Sleep tight, sweet dewlap."

Future

A dazzling sunshine,
My window ablaze;
A sparkling reflection,
The truthful mirror sells
A visionary soul.

Torrential rain and evil hail,
Clouding up a heavy head;
Reaching high, falling low,
The roller-coaster ride.

Hail the darkness, blessed light,
Will the future be so bright?
So to light up all the skies,
With forgotten stars up high.

Her Death Seems Like A Dream

Her death still seems a dream in motion,
    A fitful one at best;
No happiness here exists for me,
Much better than the rest.

It's said she's in a better place,
    "Not true at all," I say;
How can it be, 'cause I'm not there,
To caress her as she plays.

If I could only wake up once
    And steal a running glance;
To freeze a picture in my brain,
That wasn't her last dance.

The Letter

Dearest darling, precious Poochie,

I haven't talked to you
For such a very long time;
    Certainly,
Not from lack of
Thinking about you;
    My God—
    I think of little else!
Your death is still so
Very painful to me!
    I miss you so much,
Feels like you've just died,
And at the same time,
Feels like I haven't seen you in ages.
It's been forever since I held you last,
    Over ten months now.
I still can't believe that
    You're gone;
Will I ever come to terms
With your passing,
    I just don't know.
Dealing with your absence is quite
Different at the lake than
During the working months,
To put it simply,

More free time to think
About everything,
    And you!
I looked forward to work as my
Escape from the
Grief of your death,
No escapes now, darling,
    Head on, straight!
I see you here at the cabin,
    Constantly.
I talk about the wonderful and
Funny things that you did daily,
I so wish that you were with us—
Bumper loves it here.
He sat in a cage
For three, long years,
He is truly a wonderful rabbit!
If I hadn't gone to that second
Pet loss session at the Humane Society,
I'd have never saved him,
As I saved you, precious one,
    So many times,
    But in the end,
    Not enough!
    Never enough!
Was I right at the end to

Assume that you wanted to be
        Left alone?
As painful as it was,
I respected your request,
But I just had to hold you
One last time, and I did,
        My brave Poochie!
Did I make the right decision—
To let you die at home?
Please tell me that's what you wanted!
No sterile tables and
No more injections—
        To be left to die naturally,
For your time had come,
        Oh too soon!
Never got to see you grow
        Old and grey,
My beloved Poochie!
Bidsey asks about you every day,
She still sits at her table post.
Bumper even has a post behind his cage,
He's so funny,
Can't leave it unattended.
I know heaven's where you are
Right now with
Browney and Whitey, Jodie,

Timmy and Polly,
Sweetie,
Marco and Magna,
Timothy and Thumper.
Have fun playing with
All of your brothers and sisters.

Love always from,
Mom, Dad, Bidsey and Bumper

I Woke Up Now So Full Of Hope

I woke up now so full of hope,
    That one day I shall feel,
A single ray of happiness,
    The sun would kiss and seal.

It might be blessed with pastel palette,
    Like rainbows do possess;
Connective bridges to that side,
    Hearts absent of distress.

Perhaps, a snappy four-leaf clover,
    I'll chance amongst the grass;
To press it in my favourite book,
    Where good things come to pass.

No good luck here to spray us all
    With salves of sweet content;
Oppressive work stuffed with a prayer,
    Heaven's rumblings finally spent.

I'll gather pennies in my purse,
    No fountains in my habit;
I'll stock them all and one day buy
    A small white furry rabbit.

Sweet Rabbits

We don't pick out sweet rabbits,
    We sprinkle them so well,
With all their best loved garden herbs,
    Sweet clover, dandelions.

Life's abundant with such gentleness,
    A heartbeat not denied,
Our loves that span the oceans wide,
    Roll fresh with each new tide.

Inevitably, when the time has come,
    That everyone does dread;
Precious bodies wrapped solicitously,
    Hay blankets span their journey.

Goodbye

To say goodbye, complete luxury,
Opportunity, amiss;
Instead, I screamed hysterically,
While movement entered still.

A small regret is all that's kept
Within the treasure box;
For when we gather all the dust,
It overflows and drops.

That all-important farewell pass,
It's not that sweet after all,
For when I rolled the pages back,
Her diamond days were called.

The Feedings

The food is scattered on the dirt,
    He packs it in his face;
A life robust, yet oh, too brief,
    He's gone without a trace.

Besides his beauty I can see,
    Why love him now at all?
Why wish for his survival, when
    Without him, I will fall.

It's God's sweet grace, I know for sure,
    He loves them great and small,
The lessons I will take from them,
    I'll carry 'til I'm called.

Desperation No Longer Wraps Me

Desperation no longer wraps me,
Within her smothering clutches;
As if she's somehow let me go,
Allowing some room to breathe.

Forever starving for one tiny drop
Of love from comforting eyes;
It rushes over me in waterfalls,
Previously, a temporary burial.

A cool fresh rain with cleansing powers,
New life in every pool;
An awakening from a long deep sleep,
To a love that dwells in me.

Should I Collapse

Perchance be caught, should I collapse,
    Not soon enough, I hope;
Most torturous route to hit that rock,
    A life-saving heavy rope.

A gentler place to contemplate,
This temporary submergence;
Then optimistic realization,
To a swift and graceful convergence.

Where amity outweighs anxiety and fear,
    I'll lay my head to rest;
To weave a smooth road through my dreams
    Will be the ultimate test.

Shock

Shock continues to shake my ravaged walls,
    Repeatedly knocks their crown;
Remarkably surreal, intensely harsh,
    And twists them upside down.

The raping of a fragile carcass,
    That scavenger leaves such rawness
Within my skin's mean, ragged edges,
    Undeniably, the cruelest duress.

Feeds on scraps of happiness,
    It drains my emotional persistence;
Absorbs my every essence, 'til,
    Haunting screams for hallowed existence.

Moments

Suddenly,
An event cuts through time,
Like a dagger of lightning.

Reluctantly,
The painful struggle of acceptance,
Extraction of teeth that wish to remain.

Passionately,
Embracing all love within life,
All encompassing rosebushes in spring.

Dramatically,
Occurring in random fashion,
Where fairness wears blindfolds and shackles.

Her Place No Longer Sees Her

Still, my last thought when I lay my
    head down,
No longer my first thought upon awakening,
Unbelievably, not on my mind constantly,
But etched permanently in my heart.

Mortality

I feel you, me;
You felt me, be.
Days ripped through years,
'Til none to see.

This treasured time
To touch the land;
Rare speck of eternity,
One single grain of sand.

So carefully I greet them both,
The sunshine and the moon;
I'm happy if it stings my eyes
And lights my way back soon.

'Twere all so barely blessed to see,
Speak necessity of our pain;
One stretch in mere simplicity
Is paradise in the brain.

Time

An encounter on the street one day,
So barely recognizable;
I stacked my courage up in front,
And posed my query sizable.

That ending that you divvy out,
Fancy, only you are privy;
Pray, how is it that one drags on,
While others climbs aren't pretty.

One look straight through my glaring eye,
His rapid strut right by me,
As though I'd be invisible,
No answers given freely.

I never chanced by him again,
No disappointments feigning;
'Twould hurt me so to realize,
For most, continuous raining.

Strength

Just how much strength does one possess,
    Could one day I run dry;
To have one rigid fixed amount,
    All hell breaks loose, you cry!
To dwindle this commodity,
    Where would I start to look,
That I should find one generous soul,
    Or steal it from a book.

A thought that maybe in the air,
    It floats upon the breeze;
Perhaps, it dances on the snow,
    Dainty snowflakes in the freeze.
It rides a train deep in my soul,
    Especial when there's grief,
Its birth within that solid oak box,
    Oft-times, an impossible belief.

Afterlife

How lives the soul upon its death,
For contemplation of
Some knowledge that this other place
Gives comfort from above.

An ecstasy of vast proportion,
No wish for my return;
Could such a place exist for those
Who've never raged or burned.

A need for faith consumes a few,
Through all interminable sorrow;
A pure belief in quiet contrition,
An ever hopeful tomorrow.

She Died, She's Dead

Almost a year, and I still lament
And ruminate,
About what was,
And what could have been,
About what will never be again;
A yearning that won't be denied,
A longing that spans across the miles,
Remembering how I was before,
And how she was then;
Life goes on,
Only not like before.

The Scraping On My Heart

In time, the scraping on my heart,
So gently, if at all,
As raking dead leaves on the grass,
This task shall rise and fall.

The cold of night won't feel the chill,
The stars won't scream abreast;
A jubilation for the warmth,
To marvel at solitude.

No hope for such immediacy,
Would interrupt the flow,
Of purposeful reflection,
That soothes and aches to grow.

Were When The Will Was Waning

Were when the will was waning,
    From catastrophic loss;
To wrap it in a smooth, soft cloth,
    That heavy wooden cross.

And further I would take thee,
    Along some distant road,
To stuff in some deep, hidden hole,
    'Twould immensely lessen my load.

This love, so sweet, I speak of,
    Long past in this short time,
And search for this exact repeat,
    Blue skies, release some sign.

Dismissing all for only this,
    Periodically seeming palatable;
For when the mind sees fit its strength,
    Completely unimaginable.

Fame

The path of fame, out of her realm,
What purpose to her song;
The wind gusts once across the grass,
So quickly, she is gone.

What kind of understanding,
To touch it with the hand,
How doth the heart rejoice to know,
A walk through that sweet land.

But matters not, when all is done,
Glory speaks its silent words,
Few centuries calling out her name,
Morning visions of songbirds.

Friends, Not Friends

In some friends though, you'll never see
    That solitary smile,
But underneath those layers of coats,
    End days go on for miles.

And blurred together through and through,
    A congested type of fear,
That fills them up with sour milk,
    Which flows into their tears.

A sorry lot, in time they come,
    Some form of resolution;
But all the while, the story goes,
    No pleasant constitution.

Pawprints On My Heart

Those fancy footprints on the snow,
    My runners mold a keen design;
The flakes will touch the tops with white,
    Dare not erase those mystic souls.

As miles of pawprints formed her life
And danced in circles round my shape,
Ne'er never remove these marks, unique,
    Such constant pressing on my heart.

Such Sadness Wiped His
Wretched Hands

Such sadness wiped his wretched hands
Upon the depths of mine,
Previous captured in his ornery chains,
Innate hope for running design.

So softly, I did move around,
To not disturb his ground,
I shuddered as I gasped out loud,
No sunrise could be found.

A danger that indeed I'd gone
To scratch the ocean's floor;
Alas, that glorious streak of light
Had surfaced once before.

As time rolls on to understand,
He'll show his face again;
But likewise, courage I shall find,
Held captive by the pain.

Defeated

In time, all ceasing to protest,
Of that not in my reach,
When God calls out her precious name,
Undeniably, no chance for recourse.
Few bargaining powers left inside,
Pure helplessness resides
Within these walls of emptiness,
Clear layers of despair;
But when no kicks are left in me,
Mere screams, oft-times are whimpers;
A laying down, this huge defeat,
It's life that's lost once more.

Unlikely Owners

More than a few, ashamed to say,
    I'm lost in all this pain,
Of which I speak may shock you some,
    My dog has died in vain.

Our furry friends do love us more
    Than words can ever say,
And in the end, just ask one thing,
    Please remember me, my last day.

I couldn't wait to see you when
    You came from work each day,
But why'd you leave me in the rain,
    I begged and pleaded to stay.

To some, they're just like furniture,
    For conversation best;
A knowledge that this life with animals,
    Would be the ultimate test.

Well now he's gone, recognition that,
    No love for him at all;
It's far too late to be contrite,
    I've nowhere left to fall.

First Summer

That first summer, all but gone,
And my heart didn't melt
Down those harsh, mean, cold rapids,
Intense pressure certainly felt.

As the world showed its sparkles,
One brief moment, I was still;
All the while, that sorry wind blew
Through my body, full of chill.

Could I ever hope to leave
All that sadness in my hands;
Lovely birds sing forever,
And I still love this land.

Imaginations

When all the joy, long last returns,
    Deep mourning has grown thin;
Along the water's edge I stand,
    To watch the waves roll in.

In majesty, not seen before,
    So pure in crystalline sound;
Of radiance which I'd only dreamt,
    Quite magically, I'd found.

And far inside a woodland path,
    Imaginations hit their peak;
Brown eyes flew wider, a familiar speech,
    Heaven's bursting near some creek.

Not Over

It's not over yet,
Because my eyes are blind,
To the rolling of the hills,
For the solitude I can't find.

Because my ears are deaf,
To the singing in the trees,
The buzzing of the bees,
And the coolness of the breeze.

Because my senses are dead,
To the sweetness of their bodies,
The odour of their fur,
Reluctantly, my fate was decided.

On the night that she left,
This, her heaven on earth;
Someday, all find ourselves,
Many years after.

No Wrong Decision

There was no wrong decision,
Upon that fateful night,
　　To keep her from more imminent stress
Was solely my intent;
　　God's decision seemed final.
My heart wouldn't accept her fading,
　　My gut screamed out the truth,
Moving her would be too traumatic,
　　She belonged at home in this state.
"Leave me alone!" in her language she
　　told me,
　　I had always respected her needs;
Her final request was so sacred to me,
　　We watched her, so tragically, die at home.
How would I survive without her!
　　Love greater than a pearl of high price!
I live every day without her now,
　　With considerable difficulty, for sure.

For My Friend, Elizabeth

My heart cries out so loudly for you,
As you mourn your darling Butternut;
Such terrible things happen in our lives,
If only to go back,
To change them for the better.

Because we cherish them so,
We can never do enough;
It is our fervent desire to care for them,
That we try, to no avail, to protect them.

Please remember that you saved her,
So very many times in her life.
We're forced to make choices
Out of a sincere fondness,
Therefore, no decision is wrong in the end.

Butternut was your sweet bunny
And she will always be yours;
She is grateful
For all the affection that you had for her;
She continues to send her love to you
From a green pasture in heaven.

Of course, you never completely
"Get over" such a tragedy,
You learn to live with the pain;
What other choice do we have—
I am not yet ready for that other.

Sadly, your Butternut is gone,
But lives on in every rabbit
That you will adore from now on.
No, she didn't die in vain,
For the strength that you carry today,
Comes straight from her heart.

Appreciation

Different experiences with each animal,
Essential to appreciate that which each offers,
An everlasting love for our precious departed,
Transferred so gracefully to the here and now.

A Permanent Stain

I kissed you to heaven that evil of nights,
Time, a bleaker, still moment hath not,
   As bright crimson tears bled profusely
      from eyes,
A promise, you'd not be forgot.

   Remembrances constant, as sadly
      approaches
One year that death forced himself here,
   Upon this most valuable life, oh so short,
Would give up all, to spare her that fear.

   One kindness that death gave so generous,
The relinquishment of all of her pain;
   At times, it seems mine's here to stay as
My heart wears a permanent stain.

Words Be My Solace

These words, so prolific, like this be my last,
    They flowed like a river in motion;
I tried to keep up with my tears as they fell,
    And desired a very strong potion.

To drink and to have all these sad
    memories vanish,
    And give me one day's worth of peace,
Happy ones, miraculously, blend
    with the sad,
    Without those, life should rapidly cease.

So come as they may, all these rivers
    and streams,
    As they cleanse all these pores of
      this sorrow,
And likewise, continue to put pen to paper,
    I'll pray for a contented tomorrow.

The Road To Happiness

I walk this land, at times alone,
    With sorrow at my back;
When reaching this, my destination,
    Convinced to stay on track.

A journey of such vast proportion,
    Only luck in one brief time,
Such songs in glory, exaltation,
    Long last, I'll cease to pine.

I'll lay this body down to rest
    Beneath a large oak tree,
And gather acorns and some leaves
    To toss across the sea.

These seeds to promise rejuvenation,
    Of life so lost in me,
And pave the road to happiness,
    So satisfied to see.

In My Heart And In My Soul

Changes come to our lives, oh so drastic
    at times,
      Guaranteed when cold death knocks
        once more;
Glory days wrap my spirit, twisting silver
    with gold,
      Moments treasured, never held so before.

That tortured role, no longer mine,
    When traversed, thousand miles away;
In another land, to never be touched
    By me, the same today.

A gentler side, it breathes new life,
    Believed I couldn't be;
But how I'd give this all up so,
    To hold her close to me.

To truly love that which you lost,
    Some rare and precious jewel;
It softly rests upon the heart
    And mingles with the soul.

The Love, It Continues To Grow

The love, it continues to grow,
Even after the death is done;
We continue to plant those fresh seeds,
'Cause true love shines as bright as the sun.

And in time, it's the pain that we bury,
Many miles as it takes to the stars;
All the sweetness that emerges from the soul,
Weaves a cover that embraces all hours.

To Banish All Feelings

Ultimately, to banish all feelings,
    Pray knowledge, which to choose;
To rid the pain would forgo touch
    Of love to possibly lose.
Could I survive without a love,
    Defends me from my fears;
The body cold, the spirit sleeps
    Within my soul, so dear.

Time Stops

As I wonder to endure
All the pain in my life,
Deplorably ticking
So deliberate through all time;
Then the pause, and
The days are like
Thousands of years;
She was simply the best,
So sublime.
And it seems that she's gone, and
Is not coming back,
But I know that she floats in the air,
Who's the angel that colours
My rainbows so bright,
Pink and green, amber, gold,
All so fair.

I Ask You Not To Mourn For Me

I ask you not to mourn for me,
For many long, sad days;
My tired body's gone to rest,
Kept warm by sun's soft rays.

I pray, don't long for me, my dear,
Our souls are bound with twine,
By love that knows no end in sight,
A hope, forever mine.

And finally, please do live your life,
My love surrounds your soul;
For when you cry those wretched tears,
Gold memories will take hold.

So think of me, my tearful friend,
Who loved me, loved me so;
My life with you was so complete,
It took God, to make me go.

I'll Close My Eyes And Dream Of Joy

A sense of doom washes over me,
    The waves come crashing in;
She's doomed to die, but once again,
    My vision, ghastly dim.

'Tis ne'er a joyous celebration,
    A sorrowed memory at best;
All details of that deathly night,
    Faintly sharper than the rest.

Such dread, deep in my weary bones,
    The tortured week before;
I'll close my eyes and dream of joy,
    And sweetness ever more.

My eyes will always weep for her,
    The missing's so intense;
Acceptance crept so slowly in,
    No room for thin pretence.

A wish to fall asleep and wake,
    When all of this is over,
But deep inside my heart I know,
    She leads me on through clover.

She'll Never Get To Heaven

She'll never get to heaven,
If she doesn't sadly die;
It's a tragic consolation
That'll surely make you cry.

No one knows, my dear girl,
When their time finally comes;
But indeed, just as well,
When your life has been spun.

That next bursting sunrise,
'Tis not owed to us,
So enjoy your short life and
Hold back all your fuss.

Please be good to your friend,
Before their ultimate fate, since
When the morning cock crows,
It'll all be too late.

Prepared hollow speeches and
Tedious funereal chatter;
In the dim final reckoning,
They don't really matter.

So cherish every day's day,
As were it your last night,
   For that day will alas come,
When you're sure to be right.

   And lead on, sweet McDuff,
So alive, ever pretty;
   Wax on, what's been said,
In this poetical ditty.

Out Of Death's Shadow

Distant memories of that tragedy,
    Passing windows of my life;
A part of me, I won't let go,
    Sheer strength comes from the strife.

No longer dominate my thoughts,
    They flutter 'bout my head,
As birds that crash through windowpanes,
    A calamity, suddenly dead.

And broken pieces still abide,
    I've picked them one by one;
A finger pricked, some drops of blood,
    My sorrow's never done.

So here I am, I understand
    The nature of my pain;
I struggled through death's shadow where
    No longer I remain.

No More Fight In Me

My raging spirit, tranquil at last,
The fight has gone from me;
Just as her tiny body stopped,
Resolution sets me free.

Accepting death is not a choice,
She's left her earthly state;
Previously stood, my fantasy promised,
For 'round the corner stood fate.

The thorn still stabs me in the breast,
Though edges have grown round;
A cavity lies empty in my heart,
She slumbers beneath the ground.

My Darkest Hour

Alone in this, my darkest hour,
Death spirits move in close;
Stripped to the core of any peace,
Religiously waiting for something…
A distant voice calls out her message,
    Such melancholy murmurs;
    Stark reminders of her faraway cries,
    When waiting was foremost to prayer;
    And watch I will,
    'Til heaven's gaping mouth
    Shall swallow her once more.
    She can't die twice,
    But in my brain—
    A corpse,
    One thousand times.

In Memoriam

You were a blessing
Sent to me,
To love and to cherish.
For many years,
You were a part of my life,
Giving unconditional love
Every day.
You will be sadly missed—
But never forgotten.
Rest in peace,
Sweet friend.

The Panic Of Yesteryear

I sense the panic of
    Yesteryear,
Anxiety insurmountable,
To travel back and
Bravely attempt
To alter the course of time;
A different kind of therapy,
    Perhaps,
      No operations;
These notions bring
    Repeated torture
To existing twisted thoughts.
    A body separated by
        Madness,
As half seeks peace,
    The other war,
Just like some whirling dervish,
Mesmerized by the past.
How does one
Capture one's own self
Into a scathing prison;
The brain sits cold and
    Freezes, while
A wish for time to race.
    The breath I breathe,
    The life I lead,

This too, in time shall pass;
   A cry for peace,
   A gasp of air,
My time is not yet here.

She Was Alive When She Was Dying

I need to mark this day in time,
Significance so outstanding;
The day she left her sweet, green earth,
To sit on heaven's bright steps.

I need to stop and pay her homage,
Her life gave such great joy,
To all that happened in my own;
She'll never be forgotten.

I need to celebrate her life
In dying, as in living,
In crystal vision, her glory abounds,
A spirit exuding such vibrancy.

I need a soft remembrance,
Recollection of my thoughts,
Her eyes, no longer bright, went dim;
She was alive, as she lay dying,
Even my hands cried out loud.

Time Stands Still

Time stands still for me now,
The ravaging moment is eminent;
A preoccupation with her demise,
The haunting is well on its road.

A need that requires no description,
A longing so insatiable, it defies imagination;
It's no longer, "Let me hold her, one
    last time,"
But so sadly, "I know this shall never be!"

Running slow motion, to reach
    no destination,
Someone, something, always holding
    me back;
Collapsing from sheer exhaustion of this
Permanent separation,
My pain stems not from denial,
    but from reality.

Oh God, Almighty Father,
Please give me strength and courage,
To endure all this pain and suffering,
    Which I know, in time shall wane.

A Smaller Pain

I live for the day when my pain is so small,
That the feeling shall be almost nil;
When my joy is so great,
I can scream to the world,
You see, I have conquered this too.
All the stars will be brilliant,
The songs, so melodious,
My days will show promise,
Yes, I'll surely taste real victory;
Does a prize wait in store,
As I finish my race?
Ah, it's life, a pure blessing—
Staring straight at my face!

Still I Live With This Dread

Meaningful words, desperate phrases,
Hopeful thoughts, painful feelings,
How I wish they didn't need to be spoken;
A desire that I'd never discovered
    this strength,
How it pales, wish she'd never been broken.

It's a method to get on with my singular life,
As I peel back the layers of skin;
'Til at last, there's my heart still abeating,
As I pull myself up, oh so thin.

Even now as the first year is closing,
So much more that still needs to be said;
As I stare at my heart with the largest of eyes,
While I say, "Still I live with this dread!"

Both Of Us

The loss is something special, that
    You treasure as a gift;
She isn't really gone at all,
    Evil death can't form a rift.

Even though you've gone now, rabbit,
    You shall know I'll go with thee,
For if there is one, there is both of us,
    No matter who remains, so are we.

Still Lives Inside Of Me

A quivering moved, inside my ever
   tired being,
As time approached to that horrid
   day in sight;
In my mind, I hung tight to her live
   little body,
Now a year, that her eyes shined so bright.

Inside of me now lies a place in my heart,
Where she lives and she breathes with
   such zeal;
All I need is to dream and to conjure her up,
During all of those moments, I still feel.

Times still come and some refuge, I so
   desperately seek,
All amongst the most heavenly hosts;
Comforting prayers till my days, so my pain
   could soon lessen,
As I run from the haunting of ghosts.

I Didn't Completely Fade

I think I'd have faded that very first year,
If it hadn't been for Bidsey and Bumper;
    As I reached out my hand to their sweet,
       loving ways,
Distant memories surfaced swiftly of
    my Thumper.

The saint of all rabbits, the gentlest of all,
This dutch belt, he did live 'til eleven,
    As he fought deathly illness for many
       long months,
Then he gallantly flew straight to heaven.

Now my angels, safe above, oh so
       joyous they'd be
With the knowledge that I'd found
    peace at hand;
    And rejoice if they saw me, amidst
       wild flowers,
With these two, following me across this land.

She Won't Die Again

The day I've revered, now approaches
    me nigh,
A strange sense of calm does beset me;
My spirits seem neither too high nor too low,
Passing time is my greatest of allies.

Thought incessantly of her for most of
    this year,
Extreme anxiety has climbed every mountain;
I'll not live that torture of seeing her die,
She proudly guards heaven's gold fountain.

I survived this first year with the greatest
    of sorrow,
The worst, thankfully over, I can see;
I shall gracefully move with fixed courage
    and strength,
For her brave spirit lies deep inside me.

No More Days

They brought me here some time ago,
   And said I'm too much trouble;
"You didn't learn quite fast enough,
   Now go, and on the double!"

Oft-times, shadows passed 'longside
   my cage,
    Some looked, others cheerfully
      said, "Hi!"
But no one wanted me for their own,
   I cried and wondered why.

Was I too big, too old, not bright,
   What were those lame excuses?
I am an animal, not a toy,
   Do I deserve my nooses?

Then, one bright day, a man came by
   And said he'd like to take me;
My small tail wagged, I've got a home,
   They didn't just forsake me.

One sharp jab was all I felt,
   My eyes went kind of sleepy;
My heart beat once, I breathed my last,
   For no more days, they'll keep me.

Thanks to my friends who watched over me,
    And worked so helter-skelter;
I passed my days as best I could,
    In this overcrowded shelter.

I'm in heaven now, where critters go—
    No human is above me;
I found a friend who knows my name,
    Who'll unconditionally love me.

Today Is The Day That She Died

My first thought this morning,
So sadly I said,
"Today is the day that she died!"
"You know that she died every day
    of this year,"
He expressed, matter of fact,
Then he cried.

We know when we buy them,
    this one day shall be;
We realize each playtime,
    a celebration in store;
We know when we feed them,
    such delightful content,
But, we know when we love them,
    shall be evermore!

Couldn't Love Her Anymore

I couldn't love her anymore,
The greatest gift from God;
I couldn't give her anymore,
The best of every measure;
I couldn't spend more time with her,
Gave meaning to my life;
My single wish, that I'd have saved her,
Such ecstasy in pleasure!

I Was Really "Up" Today!

I live my days now, with the greatest
    appreciation;
      She, so amiably graced my life for
        five years.
My capacity to love with complete fervency,
    'Twas for sure, no mean hardship with
      this dear.

The sun with her long, golden fingers
    came out,
      And caressed me in warm loving ways;
Her ever healing magic brought these
    happier thoughts,
      Inspiration, for more hopeful days.

The sky showed such beauty, her coat, clarity,
    Indulgence, as her blue melted out
Lamented moods and past tribulations,
    That I couldn't, without a doubt.

Finally, clouds spread their wings
And an archway was formed,
    Life's begun in a multitude of fashions;
I will walk with my head facing up
    to the stars,
      And I'll love with the rarest of passions!

With Her Love, I Just Know
I Can Do This

I thought that they'd find me still
Kicking and screaming,
As that day of great sorrow rolled again;
In my way, I have witnessed
Some semblance of order,
In my life, some assurance, that I'm sane.

When she died, no belief in utter recovery,
Lest a day when my spirits could rise;
As I think of her now with my greatest
    of memories,
It's a start, I've some comfort in this size.

I shall always feel sadness within
    my confines,
The missing grows stronger than ever;
In death, she became such a huge part of me,
With her love, I just know I can do this.

Ten-Fifteen

Ten-fifteen, a year later
With the sign of the cross,
   Calm,
Unlike the hysteria of her death;
Now a loving goodbye,
Too demented to say,
As for now, a trickling of tears.

At times, I believed that I'd used them
   all up,
Could a poor soul like me become stoic?
Well, my tears still flow freely,
Only not quite as often;
Dramatically,
They burst without warning.

A remembrance in order,
This sacred of days,
As the veil is removed from my eyes;
I'll shut them so tight so this moment
   can pass,
Unlike, the time that death stole her.

A Prayer

May you always rest in peace,
    My darling;
May you sing with the angels
And the heavenly hosts;
May you never go hungry,
    Never be lonely,
Always remember that I love you,
That I miss you immensely,
That I shall never forget you.
Lastly, may you always
    Be happy,
Forever and ever,
    Amen

Some Nights When My Sleep
Is A Stranger

Some nights when my sleep is a stranger,
    My thoughts tumble, scrape and
       they bleed;
There's no peace, it seems, with my grief now,
    Death revels, an insatiable greed.

It picks all our best at the worst as,
    The timing is never a bother;
Oh, let's make a deal and we'll bargain,
    And maybe, just please choose another.

Who knows who will go when, and just how,
    A life cut too short caused by quotas;
Those left with such pain endure losses,
    Our memories seem, sort of, to hold us.

The sun, she shall rise now and next time,
    And the wind will continue to blow;
It is nature, our symphony of reminders,
    It's so hard to be listening and to know.

For the long life we seek and we strive for,
    It exacts a price, much too high,
As we live out our years, to our horror,
    We get to see all our friends die.

You'll never get over the grim, grey, sad day,
So progressively worse, don't you see!
No plan cauterizes all the pain that we feel,
'Til our end sets us free, sets us free.

Ode To Life

This day shall never pass this way,
These moments, held not the same;
Our time on earth, an ivory pearl,
Death once, life a million times over.
Oh to cherish every moment
held so dearly,
And to live every day, be your last;
Special joys,
I shall paint with the brightest of colours,
Clearly visions for my mind and my heart.

Every Day That Passes By

Every day that passes by,
　　Missing rises one degree;
As the sun magnificently appears,
　　I feel her soothing warmth;
As the leaves turn brown and amber,
　　The anniversary does approach;
Pitter, patter against my windowpane,
　　Sore reminders of hopping movements.
As the days grow white and frosty,
　　Her footprints in the snow;
When she rests her golden eyes,
　　Lonely nights yearn for her presence.

She Didn't Have To Die So Soon

She didn't have to die so soon,
    She couldn't live forever;
To come to terms that one day she would
Leave me like the others.

Dear to my heart, too close to my soul,
    So painful a reality;
I'd hoped that she'd least live 'til ten,
What harm was there in dreaming.

Love Grew Deeper

When all I need's been said and done,
When loved ones have been buried;
I'm moving like a ship to sea,
A boat without its anchor.

I'm lost inside familiarity,
I seek to find some bearings,
Caught in a world of then and now,
Like living in two cities.

I used to count the weeks that passed,
So quickly, slowly through me;
Each monthly anniversary caught me,
Stuck within her tombstone.

As I pass through these pieces of time,
With an emptiness full of her lifelines,
I rejoice in the fact, my capacity to love
Has grown, much deeper and higher.

Best Friends Are Forever

I've left you in body,
But oh how my spirit
Sings only the love that you gave me;
And still, I feel warmth of your
Loving words to me,
Your poems make my heart fully swell.
My life, it did end so abruptly,
I watched as you suffered so openly;
Well, please dry your tears
So that I can dry mine,
Remember, best friends are forever.

The Mind And The Heart

The mind understands what the heart
    does so covet,
The memory, it shall never get rest;
It tries hard to forget certain points of
    great pain,
A chagrin, such a constant day's test.

Along with sore memories come
    happy ones, all,
These sing with some hope up ahead;
Just remember, face up to your suffering, so
Your future can move in good stead.

Dying's So Short

It's the dying we fear,
For this death, a mere second,
A small moment, plucked
From our existence.
Death, you've no importance,
As you couldn't snuff all
Of the love that she had inside her.

It's Been A Year And I Still Miss Her

The missing just goes on and on,
    From sunrise, then she sets;
    An image branded on my brain,
    The greatest, no regrets.

I celebrate the joys we had,
    That I have known real love;
    Oh yes, I loved, and yes I gained,
    Vital lessons for my life.

To Thumper

He came one day, so fine and clear,
    His eyes, they were so shiny and dear;
One ear was brown, the other white,
    The days, so filled with joy and delight.

He loved to race around the room,
    And oh, the fun when he did groom;
He loved to dig on quilts of fluff,
    But never, was there a bunny so tough.

Finally, nothing lasts forever, you know,
    So keep that in mind as they live
        and they grow;
The end was painful, but he never left,
    He stayed in our hearts and quietly slept.

The Gift Of Love

I ache from the depths of my soul for
    her touch,
Could a dream offer comfort from a glimpse;
The death is so easy, it's the life that's so hard,
I just want to see her, here with me.
Forever searching for the recipe,
That could give me some rest, and
Some peace at the end of the tunnel.
It lies with the love, this great gift that
    she gave,
To my heart and my soul and my life.

My Sorrow's A Constant Companion

The pain is always there,
It won't leave me alone,
Sometimes, so close at hand,
Other times, just around the corner,
But always within my reach.
Some days, like a feather,
It brushes my face;
Other days,
It stabs me so violently,
Reminders of the day
That changed my life forever,
That took her away from me.
I suppose he's become
A persistent friend;
Without this sorrow,
She'd have never existed.
This severity though,
Thrives on pushing me to my limits,
Encouraging me to feel
All that life has to offer.

I Shall Never Forget…

I shall never forget—
The sweetness of your face,
The softness of your fur,
The brightness of your eyes;
Your playful personality.

I shall always remember—
The happiness that we shared,
The way you licked my nose,
Your dancing when I fed you;
Your unconditional love.

I shall always treasure—
Your first day with us,
Your toughness during illness,
Your last day on this earth;
Your glorious life with us.

Once In A While, A Day Comes Along

Once in a while, a day comes along,
That seems to come together;
Even my sorrows boast of long
    waited healing,
No weight, you're as light as a feather.

When songs play so gently on the tips
    of your lips,
As you strut through the crunch of
    fall leaves;
Squirrels in staccato, up and down
    bare tree branches,
All the while, my thoughts still do weave,

In and out, joyful memories mixed
    with melancholia,
Her life, like a singular strand of pearls,
That I'll wear with great pride as they rest
    on my skin,
As did whiskers, countless times,
    oddly curled.

Death Knows Not The Heart

On such a day, no one be sick,
A time for health and laughter;
To wrap all worries in a chest,
Sweet play for here and after.

Illness knows not of the weather,
Sadness needs valuable time,
Seasons turn in delegated order;
Despicable death knows of nothing—
Death knows not the heart.

Even The Most Unpleasant Garden Must Be Tended

We rummage in the rubbish heaps of others,
While our own fertile paradise
    remains unattended;
Our kind seems at times, not to belong,
Coins jangle in our pockets,
No thought to what cost these trinkets;
Our destructiveness seems unstoppable,
And so on and so forth.

A cat needs not nine lives—
Only one.
Our vanity is boundless,
Along with our viperous capacity
    for opulence.
Our dilettante rags and potions cost
    countless pelts and pain,
And so it goes.

The soul speaks out when we torture,
And we know;
But like the thorn birds, impale ourselves,
Again and again.

The creatures we live with cannot speak out,
The home, they must share with us,

We must share with them;
They are not gadgets to play with,
And discard at a whim.

We must not spit on their souls.
We must honour our chair.

Confrontation

To look death in the face without screaming,
    Is a feat I shall never achieve;
To look life in the face, fully rejoicing,
    I shall do 'til my last breath.

The Flowers In Their Feet

So gracefully, they groom themselves,
Very regularly with such style;
Always licking fur,
Joyously stroking ears,
Cleaning faces like tiny babies;
When they stretch those
Huge, hind feet,
Awaiting you, fantastic surprises,
They spread their toes
Forming a furry flower
In every grooming round.

And Most Of All, I'll Miss Her Eyes

And most of all, I'll miss her eyes,
Those sweet brown orbs that spoke volumes
In silence;
Those accepting eyes.

They once radiated her love
For us;
And the spark of life
That danced on those trusting spheres,
Graced our lives.

When death whispered,
It's time to go,
She quietly said goodbye,
And the spark went out.

The ceremony was brief,
Her candle was spent,
Those eyes were clouded now
    with death's milk.

I passed my hand over her tiny head—
And her eyes closed;
Those beautiful eyes,
Forever.

Her suffering was gone,
And she seemed to be smiling;
An angel carried her spirit away,
And even as the tears streamed
     down my cheeks,
I saw her eyes open in heaven.

I Never Thought I'd Be Happy Again

I'm alive to feel the pain of loss,
And the joys that comfort me in their arms;
One day, I won't feel anything.
'Til then, I will marvel at all that life gives me;
Let it bite my face in the dead of winter,
Let it burn my skin in the heat of summer,
As it quenches a tree's thirst on a
    thunderstorm night,
Glorious puddles for small boys to play in.
    I shall nurture, love and respect all
      my animals,
I shall cherish my dear husband, always.
I shall celebrate each blessed day that I wake,
And thank God that He gave me a life.

Realization

Once you realize that,
One day, you will feel
Neither pain nor joy,
You shall achieve
Meaning in your life.

Surprises All Around

Surprises all around for me,
No thoughts of sorrow for hours;
Oh blessed day, you've finally come,
Just how long will you stay!

Funeral For A Bird

I found a dead bird on the curb,
Before stopping at the bakery after work.
I asked the lady for a favour,
"May I have a bag to move him
To a nicer place, so that his spirit might soar,
Like it did once before his demise."
He was small with a pale yellow belly,
Had a black back, speckled with white.
I gently picked him up and put his limp body
Into the double paper bags;
Later, removed the little ball of feathers,
Respecting his fragility,
Placed him under a small tree,
Beside the river, behind my home.
Then, decided to rest him on a large leaf,
Picked him up again, and some
Dried leaves stuck to his sticky feathers,
So covered him with another leaf—
Then, the funeral began;
Cried, the "Our Father," to honour his life—
Waited a moment in reverence.
Then said, "I'm sorry, I don't know your name,
Sweet bird, so sorry, you won't fly again!
Your wings won't ever taste the soft breezes;
    May I beg of you a small favour—
Would you please sing to her in heaven!"

The Last Time That I Saw Her Face

I still remember the moment,
    That I held my Poochie,
    For the very last time.
Catharine, one of her doctors,
Ever so gently had asked
To have her body;
    The first time,
    I wasn't ready,
I would never be ready.
After one hour of holding her
Tightly against my chest,
I realized the inevitable;
Tears clouded my vision,
My speech dissolved,
Catharine cradled her in her arms,
Out of my sight forever.
    She was gone…
If I didn't die at that exact moment,
I was far-off from alive
As I drove home with my husband;
No memory of that ride home.
Life would never be the same.
    One year later,
The truth be known.
    It never was.
    It never will be.

I Kick The Leaves

I kick the leaves and think out loud,
    That nothing lives forever.
She's in an urn, a pink flowered urn,
    As she was, I'll never have her.

Some tears come as they often do,
    I'd surely love to see her,
So dear and close, a friend was she,
    Pray tell, why can't she be here?

Life, we cannot give or take,
    Enjoy it, while you have it;
For when it's gone, its flame blown out,
    You'll have no chance to grab it.

Tears are spent on those we've lost,
    Their return is not an issue;
They can't be here, be here, be here,
    To tell us, they too, miss you.

So, recall, recall, those sweet old times,
    Death's sting hurt once at best;
Our tears are truth to wash the sad,
    Our love will do the rest.

Empty Bowl, Empty Heart

A peaceful sleep came to her heart,
    It comes to all, we know;
But why her, even now I ask,
    Did she really have to go?

I know, I know, there comes a time
    When all of us must part;
Such thoughts are of no help at all,
    Her empty bowl, my empty heart.

My loss, my love, my pain goes on,
    I sure do miss her touch;
So quietly, I pray and know,
    She loves me just as much.

We never get over those we've loved,
    Our grief can even grow;
No plastic plan can soothe the loss,
    That's how it is, you know.

Her spirit shines forevermore,
    I take strength from all its light,
Until we meet again, sweet bear,
Sweet dreams and sweet good night.

Her Song

De Camptown ladies sing dis song,
Dew-lap! Dew-lap!
De Camptown race track five miles long,
Oh! De dew-lap day!
'Gwine to run all night!
'Gwine to run all day!
I'll bet my money on de bob-tail nag,
Somebody bet on de bay.

(Adapted from a song by Stephen Foster;
some of the lines have been changed to
celebrate her gorgeous and fluffy dewlap).

Bruce's Cat

His eyes light up when
She does a Bucky thing;
She sleeps under his bed,
He knows exactly where she is,
Especially when she rolls on her side,
And takes a little nap
In the cradle formed by his arm.
She's his cute little girl,
Buckminster's the full name,
After some architect.
Lately, he calls her "baby",
Her wonderful feet,
Her tiny little feet,
Her dainty feet,
Her gentle presence;
She's so expressive,
Her pretty head tilts and
She knows fully what he means,
Particularly when he says,
"Bye, bye."
She waits so patiently
On his studio chair
For him to return.
On weekends, he's a
Sleeper inner;
The cat knows and

Loves him anyway.
She even puts up with his
Rough-housing,
The price she pays for all the food
And love,
He delightfully gives to her.
She knows she's loved,
Of course she is,
She's Bruce's cat.

She Lost Everything

She left this world, no comfort zone,
Negation, my signature touch;
Willful effort bestowed by God
To love her 'til the end.

So lovingly, I positioned myself
In line, horizontally with her.
But, she scurried to solitary state,
This signal was her farewell.

The breath that I had held so dear,
It ebbed before my eyes;
Her life, all love, it pained her so,
My sweet, you did lose everything.

No One Told Me How It Would Be

Another lifetime now,
A million miles away;
She lived and breathed and loved
With such earnestness;
My eyes beheld phenomenal surprise!

Never knowing how it would be,
No one told me what to do;
Following instincts within
An anguished body,
I did what I felt I had to do,
To make myself feel better,
If that was even possible.

No rules for grief, no timelines,
And still a need to know,
What others did and what they felt,
To bring back wholeness and sanity,
To work through pain and sadness.

The mystery, invariably, still remains,
When life ends, death begins;
The answers cannot bring her back,
No answers even exist.

If There Is A Hell, I Was There

If there is a hell,
I was there for a while,
When all life froze in front
Of my body, that no longer
Cried for life.

Such a pain reduced
From my memory now,
As shrinking threads
Squeeze a heart,
No longer tear.

All wounds have been sewn,
One by one,
Such perfection in this mending;
While deep scars
Form striations,
Invisible to the world,
But not to me.

So to never forget where such
Torture had its birth;
So to always remember,
Certain pains find their death.

Recovery

You must recover,
Somehow, someday;
They will all go—
Every last one of them,
To a God who will love them
Just as much,
To a place where illness will
Never again touch them,
To a comfort of the
Greatest proportion,
That shall ease any lingering
Degree of pain;
To a new life that will
Deny them
Nothing.

A Poem For A Child

I'm so sorry that your friend has died!
What was his name?
Was he very sick?
It's all right to cry, you know.
Your pet was a friend to play with
And take care of.
Real animals sometimes get sick,
Veterinarians take care of them.
Sometimes, your pet may become too sick
For even the vet to keep him alive.

Your pet will die one day and
You will feel very sad and lonely;
You will miss him very much.
Crying will help you to feel better;
You may even feel angry and
Wonder why your best little friend
Had to die.

You may want to know more about dying,
So it's important to ask your Mom or Dad,
Or a friend
To answer your questions.
Dying isn't like sleeping,
Your pet will never wake up.
It's all right to see your

Pet's body after he dies—
To stroke his fur or feathers
And kiss him goodbye.

Having a funeral for your pet
Will help you to deal with the end
Of his life.
His body can be placed in a box and
Buried in the ground or
Sometimes an animal's body is burned
And the ashes are kept in a small urn,
A special bottle for ashes.
You can keep this urn at home or
You can bury it.
You can even sprinkle his ashes
In your favourite garden
Or a place where your friend liked to be.
Saying some special things about him,
Telling everyone why you loved him,
Is a nice way to say goodbye.

You may need to be alone for a while,
But remember, you will not always
Feel bad about the death of your friend.
Talk about this with someone you love,

They will understand how badly you
    are feeling.
Putting the pictures of your pet
Into an album will help you
To remember all of the good times.
You may even want to
Write about him in a little poem or story.

One day, you will feel happy again,
And you may even want another pet.
Happy and sad times are a part of
Everyone's life.
The love you had for you pet will
Live inside of you forever.

Celebrations, At Last

Still lie small shades of ample guilt,
Where happiness has seeped
Inside those places, I revealed,
Holding comfort and real joy!

That I should not, how could I have
Displayed these demonstrations,
Where laughter bubbles vibrantly,
That I can even sing.

To not mistake these recent pleasures,
Confusion met its death;
At last, I celebrate her presence,
For five years, mirrored mine.

The Heart Of My Life

No, I shan't look straight back
From this distance that I came,
Except where loving memories
Now do beckon me,
Misty visions, soulful dancing in
The cool of my nights
Offer breath in the clear of the day.

Silhouettes haunt, enchant precious
Footsteps from her life,
Excessiveness captures my brain
In her raptures,
Sweet, candied words take my lips
For a ride,
Squeezing remnants of fleeting pain
From my edges.

Continuance of discovery, countless
Reasons for my muse,
Only now, that dark casket,
Almost hollow,
'Cause her wings take her deep to the
Heart of my life,
Gratefully acceptance, where daunting
Disturbance once existed.

To Love Another

I didn't want another rabbit,
After my precious girl died;
I only wanted her back.
But that couldn't be, so
The time came to save another.
There will always be others to rescue.
Remember, animals
Are often abandoned.
You can give an animal a home,
Giving you some hope—
A new friend.
You will love your departed pet
Forever;
I still miss mine.
I will always miss her.
The time to give love to
Another dear will come.
You have an endless source of love;
Perhaps, you will find
Some happiness again.
I adopted a beautiful rabbit, who
Sat in a cage for a very long time.
He races, jumps and twirls
Every day of his life;
Happiness has embraced
Both of us.

Will I Know When It's Time

Will I know when it's time?
Will I know when the Rainbow Bridge
Has saved a nest for you
And called you one final time?

Oh Thumper, I knew the moment had come;
Seven months of careful hand feedings,
Daily steroids to boost your strength,
And aspirin to aid your arthritic legs.

Misery, still foreign to your gentle soul,
A voracious appetite welcomed my mornings,
A tongue that loved my face,
As I washed your disease-ravaged body,
And ears, such antenna tendencies,
Excited with every sound.

We watched you so patiently endure
Weeks of heart pills and diuretics.
One morning, no longer bright,
Your eyes said it all.

"Mom, it's just too hard—
Fun no longer visits me;
I must say goodbye
To all my friends.

I need respite from all of this,
I long for the soft lap of comfort;
Please cradle me the way you do
And always remember,
I love you,
It's time."

I made the call.

Did you know where we were going,
On the highway, three minutes from
    the needle,
Under the power line, in a field of alfalfa,
Cradled in my arms,
Your smooth pink nose and different
    coloured ears
Twitched for the very last time,
And the angels caught your soul.

There Will Only Be One Of Her

My grief was inconsolable
This morning.
I cried and cried when it hit me,
So severely, just why
I had to write this book;
Letting it go on this final road,
Felt like giving her body up,
One more time.
Completely unbearable!
I am fully spent.
My eyes burn,
My head aches,
My love is undying,
And I know that
I cannot, will not,
Ever give her up…
Completely.

'Til Storms No Longer Blow

Depleted as I raise myself
Up from the former well,
Denied of that exquisite life,
Restored to newer ground.

The shroud has dropped
So far away,
Its weight, no longer pulling
Upon my sore fragility,
Inside my damaged heart.

No lies live here upon my road,
For stings do punctuate,
And make a toasty moment frosty,
That rip my repaired seams,

And flood my quiet,
Sombre screaming
With numerous explosions,
That make their routine circuit round,
'Til storms no longer blow.

Nostalgia

Remembering my then and now,
Vivid images flash through my being;
A strobe light spins out of control,
Happy and sad, celebrations, departures.

Goodbye feels so clearly irreverent,
Remains all desire to go back in time;
Questioning this state of acceptance,
Always travelling through that familiar tunnel.

Only now a light glows cheerfully,
Lively imaginations left, but two steps back—
And dreams do reach the ultimate pedestal,
Don't ask, heaven knows not its bounds.

And Songs Are Locked Away 'Til Never

I still yearn where no one can see,
A soul stripped beyond recognition—
Where benevolent hearts shatter too easily
And songs are locked away 'til never.

I've no sacred place left to hide,
My secrets now breathe wholesome air—
I'm clutching dancing rainbows in my hands,
Swiftly riding with the man in the moon.

Would she know me if she
Came back for one long moment—
This briefness would be my forever.
I could spot her were she a blade of grass,
Were a flower amidst her sisters
Or a single grain of sand.

I would climb the highest hilltop
And swim the deepest waters,
To catch one fantastic glimpse of her
Ears waving to me, miles from my existence.

Laughter

Good laughter sends me to the sea
To bathe, her baptismal waves;
To wrap myself within her distance,
A form of carnal oblivion
From all that ails a murky existence.

Repetitive movements,
Such forceful arms
Keep pace, as magical music
Resounds deep inside my head,
Fiercely vigorous and buoyant
And steams me on again.

The wailings gone, a sadness lingers,
So determined, I push on
As sounds so gently squeeze
My depths,
Finally resting on my tongue
As words selected and spun.

For all that I have seen and done,
The pictures still remain,
A vividness, formerly razor sharp
Has softened tattered edges;
I've cushions now to breathe,
Her billows carry me quietly to sleep.

Love Knows Not Of This Death

Love knows not of this death, so rampant,
She breathes life of her own;
Does throb when hearts have ceased to beat,
Her love does revel beyond loving.

She cannot see an end in sight,
So cherishes her beginning,
And gratitude for this infinite continuance,
Love lives, all powerful, forever.

Love waits to touch all precious tomorrows,
Sunrises and sunsets,
She fashions herself to all these rhythms
That move in singular direction.

Love imagines not to waste herself
On superficial existence,
But finds a place within the hearts
Of those exuding sincerity.

Love capitulates herself to those
Holding welcome in their arms,
Who'll cradle affection in their warmth,
Who'll love her 'til their death.

When Only The Love Remains

All the love I had,
I gave to you,
And you the same to me.
You let me into your life,
And touched me—
Helping me in ways
That you will never know.
I experienced the very best of you,
Your incredible love of life,
Your quiet strength,
And courage in difficult times,
Your beautiful, affectionate self;
You let me get so close to you—
You really loved me—
Like no one ever had!
You were playful, mischievous,
And demanding;
I loved absolutely everything about you!
I welcomed you with open arms,
Because I knew the sad reality,
That one day, you'd be gone.
Well, that day has come—
I can't bear one single moment
Without you!
I will cry for a very long time.
But already, beautiful memories

Rush one after the other
Through my mind constantly—
So many gratifying moments,
I cannot begin to count them.
Your pain is over,
That alone must give me
Some relief.
Now, only the love remains.
You can sleep now.
Rest in peace, my darling,
Love always.

Note from the author:

If you have any comments about this book or would like to share your experiences with the author, she would love to hear from you. Let her know if her poems have helped you to face your pain and deal with your loss. She can be reached at the following address:

Emily Margaret Stuparyk
1107-246 Roslyn Rd.
Winnipeg, MB. R3L OH2
Canada

Please include a self-addressed, stamped envelope, if you wish to receive a reply.